A MILLION LITTLE MIRACLES

A MILLION LITTLE MIRACLES

A COMMON SENSE INTRO TO
THE LAW OF ATTRACTION

LISA KENTNER

NEW DEGREE PRESS

COPYRIGHT © 2023 LISA KENTNER

All rights reserved.

A MILLION LITTLE MIRACLES

A Common Sense Intro to the Law of Attraction

ISBN   979-8-88504-449-3 *Paperback*
           979-8-88504-492-9 *Hardcover*
           979-8-88504-473-8 *Ebook*

To Rachel,

*My very best miracle.
May all your wishes
become your reality.
Dream big!*

CONTENTS

PREFACE	1
INTRODUCTION	5
WHAT IS THE LAW OF ATTRACTION?	15
GET YOUR HEAD RIGHT	23
WHAT ARE YOUR THOUGHTS ON THE LAW OF ATTRACTION?	33
COINCIDENCES, SIGNS, AND SYNCHRONICITIES	43
HOW TO USE THE LAW OF ATTRACTION—MONEY	53
HOW TO USE THE LAW OF ATTRACTION—CAREER	63
HOW TO USE THE LAW OF ATTRACTION—RELATIONSHIPS	73
THE LAW OF ATTRACTION AND DISEASE	83
MANIFESTING THINGS	87
MANIFESTING PEOPLE	95
EIGHT THINGS I'VE LEARNED ABOUT THE LAW OF ATTRACTION	105
CHOOSE JOY	115
ACKNOWLEDGMENTS	123
APPENDIX	125

PREFACE

Five years ago, my husband lost his job because of a lapse in judgment. The job loss, lack of jobs available in his field, and his identity tied up in his job impacted his mental health. He was in a very dark place. I was worried about him and was desperately searching for a way to help him feel better about himself.

In a networking group, I met a woman who shared her story of poor past relationships and how she discovered the law of attraction. She and her husband were hosting an introductory workshop on how to use the law of attraction. I spent $300 that we didn't have and signed both of us up for the upcoming workshop. Normally, he would have fought me about going, out of concern we were spending too much money. But this time, even he knew we needed help.

The following Saturday, we headed to the 9:00 a.m. Law of Attraction Workshop. The first thing we learned was that everything is at a vibrational level and that like attracts like. We explored how as a couple and individually we had been thinking negatively about ourselves and how we didn't have enough money. Throughout the day, we were given exercises about moving our vibrational levels from depression up the spectrum to joy. The process that really stuck with me was that when the feeling of lack kicked in, the best thing to do was write a list of things I was grateful for. This exercise has stuck with me, and I continue to use it daily.

After the workshop, my husband seemed better and was working hard at finding a new job. He carried a more positive energy level, his eyes had some of the old sparkles, and there seemed to be a hopefulness instead of the dread before the workshop. He was in contact with two companies about potential jobs. We were living in Michigan, and the first job would involve travel to Illinois, Wisconsin, Michigan, and Ohio. The other job was with a CPA firm that would involve travel in just Ohio and Michigan and was very similar to the job he had just lost, and it was his first choice. The problem was that they didn't have his position in their budget for the current year.

It was a Saturday, September 25, and we were coming home from a friend's birthday party around midnight. As my husband was driving us home, a car with a vanity license plate that read 1119CPA passed us.

I smacked my husband's arm and said, "You are going to end up with your first-choice job with the CPA firm on November 19."

Rubbing his arm where I had smacked him, he said, "Wouldn't that be weird?"

I told him, "It won't be weird. It is the law of attraction at work, and the Universe is giving us a sign that everything will work out."

I truly, truly knew he was going to get that job.

Fast forward to November. My husband received an offer on his second job choice. He was worried the other job, his first choice, wouldn't come through and accepted his second-choice job.

I told him, "Call your first-choice job and let them know you could wait until January for the job if they would put the offer in writing."

He listened and did contact the company to explain his situation. He received the offer letter from his first-choice company on November 19. The driver's license plate we saw in September was a sign from the Universe. The law of attraction worked for me, and I was on my way to becoming a true believer.

INTRODUCTION

―

"Belief is a wise wager. Granted that faith cannot be proved, what harm will come to you if you gamble on its truth, and it proves false? If you gain, you gain all; if you lose, you lose nothing. Wager then, without hesitation."

—BLAISE PASCAL

What if there was a way to get everything you wanted in life just by changing the way you think? Would you take the time to read, listen, and practice? Are you willing to invest the time in you?

My goal is to help you start living your dream life by giving you the basics—a common sense strategy on how to get started using the law of attraction to live your best life. What is the law of attraction? The law of attraction supports that our thoughts (positive or negative) attract experiences of the same energy to come into our lives. In other words, "like attracts like."

I am a Midwest girl, the eldest daughter of a plumber and a bookkeeper who taught me I could do anything I wanted if I put my mind to it and worked. They also taught me to have fun and enjoy the ride. I am also a mom, sister, business owner, aunt, friend, and true believer in the law of attraction. I am a practical person who is a problem solver for my clients and friends. My secret weapon is that I am focused and self-disciplined (some areas are better than others). I love when people doubt me because I will use that to my advantage and do everything in my power to prove them wrong.

I am writing this book to introduce the law of attraction and help people learn to use it so they can improve their existence and live the life of their dreams. The most tumultuous year of my life was 2021, and I know I wouldn't have made it through as well as I did without using the law of attraction. Going through a divorce is a great way to challenge your love of yourself and your mental stability.

Super Bowl Sunday will forever be the day I learned I was going to get a divorce. My ex informed me he wasn't happy, didn't want to live this way, blah, blah, blah. I won't bore you with the nitty-gritty details other than to share that after he delivered his speech, I knew I needed to get away from him and think. My thoughts were going 100 miles a minute, and I felt like I had lost control. I clearly remember looking out the bathroom window and talking to my sister on the phone. She asked if I wanted to fly to Houston to get away. I didn't think I could book an airline ticket, which is difficult enough to do when I have all my faculties about me.

Instead, I decided to drive to my hometown to see my parents. My sister, who was also another reason I made it through the year, called my parents for me to tell them what was happening and let them know I was headed their way.

Parents never stop being parents. They never stop worrying about us, and they always, always wish the best for us. I grew up in Illinois, and I know the eight-hour drive from Michigan by heart. I figured the long drive would give me time to process the thought of going through a divorce.

I quickly packed a bag and threw my computer in the car to get on the road as soon as possible.

The drive involved tears, mostly about how my daughter's life would change and my fear of the financial aspects of living in a separate household. The money worries created a huge pit in my stomach. I knew what I made, and going through the costs of keeping a home running made me want to throw up between the tears. I also felt bad for my daughter, who didn't know anything about the divorce at this time. My parents were divorced when I was an adult, and trying to split the holidays between them always leaves me feeling that when I am at one house, I should be at the other. Trying to make the visits equal was something I didn't want her to have to deal with. Looking back, I did not have a single thought about how I would live without my husband, which gives an indication of the relationship.

Early in the drive, I pictured myself at a fork in the road. One path would have been temporarily easy. That path involved lots of junk food, pajamas, a big box of Kleenex, and a pity party for one. The other path involved me putting on my big girl panties, keeping my head down, focusing on what I wanted, taking care of myself, and setting a great example for my daughter, teaching her that in life we can get knocked down, but the important part is that we don't stay down. We pop back up to show the world we are strong, resilient, and will come out better on the other side of our challenges. Those challenges teach us lessons, help us to be more empathetic, humble, and, most importantly, grow and get closer to realizing our dreams.

My law of attraction knowledge kicked in almost immediately. I knew I would have to take care of myself during this process with exercise, eating right, sleeping—or trying to sleep—and that I would need to call in the troops. The first thing I did was plug in an audio book, *Make Room for Joy: Choose Hope and Cultivate Joy in the Middle of Life's Most Complicated Seasons*, by Vanessa Joy Walker.

I don't remember much, but I do remember that Vanessa said good things will come from difficult times (Walker 2020). Before learning about the law of attraction, I probably would have spent a large time at the pity party for one. After studying and learning about the law of attraction, I knew I couldn't live in a state of depression.

So, my commonsense brain started making a list of good things that would come from the divorce. One, I wouldn't have to worry about what was wrong with the marriage. Two, no more dealing with all the stuff that led up to the divorce. Three, I would buy the most beautiful, colorful bedspread when I was divorced. I wouldn't have to consult anyone, and no more neutral-colored geometric patterns for me. It could be as girly as I wanted. So, I really focused on my future bedspread. It sounds crazy, but it made me happy. It was also a way to keep my mind from heading to negative thoughts and all the possible things that could happen. If I pictured myself homeless or living in a dumpy apartment, I would snap that thought out of my mind by picturing my beautiful new bedspread.

Why is it so easy for our minds to go directly to negative thoughts or the worst-case scenario? According to Kendra Cherry's article in *Verywell Mind*, "Research has shown that across a wide array of psychological events, people tend to focus more on the negative as they try to make sense of the world. Additionally, studies have shown that negative news is more likely to be perceived as truthful. Since negative information draws greater attention, it also may be seen as having greater validity. This might be why bad news seems to garner more attention" (Cherry 2022).

I had to acknowledge my feelings and that things were going to change and then jump into action. I was going to be a single parent with a daughter who was headed to college in a couple of years. I didn't want her to see me give up. I wanted to teach her that life throws us curveballs, and we might not like it, but it is always better to move forward than give up. So, with eyes swollen from crying, deeply sad, embarrassed, and pissed, I wasn't sure what was going to happen but knew I would get through the divorce. I always look at situations I am in, and if others have gotten through those tough things, I figure I can too. According to the CDC, there were 630,505 divorces and annulments in the US in 2020, which means about 45 percent of all marriages end in divorce (US Department of Health & Human Services 2020). I play games in my head, and if forty-five out of one hundred people got divorced and survived, I knew I could do it too. But I wanted to thrive, not just survive. I would have to make myself a priority, which isn't part of a mom's nature.

When I arrived at my mom's house, there were more tears. She was 100 percent on my side and would help me however she could. I told her good things would come from the divorce. At first, she looked at me like I had gone crazy, which, let's be honest, had happened a few times on my eight-hour drive to Illinois. Several items on the list made her laugh. The last item I told her was that I was going to get the prettiest bedspread I could find when I was divorced. Then I thought, why wait? I was going to find the bedspread in the very near future.

My mom, bless her heart, is one of those people whose house is always decorated for the holidays. She changes her decor with the seasons or her mood, including bedspreads. I am more like my grandmother; I use a bedspread until it wears out. Anyway, my mom had a lightbulb moment and told me she had bought a beautiful bedspread, but she didn't like how it looked with her carpet and didn't think she had donated it because it was really nice.

She asked me, "Do you want to go look for it?"

Since I had nothing to do except think about my upcoming divorce, I said, "Sure."

We entered her very large walk-in closet and looked on the top shelves where there were several garbage bags full of multiple bedspreads. About the fourth bag in, my mom pulled out an absolutely gorgeous bedspread with a watercolor feel of beautiful big flowers in purples, creams, and greens that looked like they were blowing in the wind. The fabric was a really soft cotton. My husband would have hated it, and I loved it!

My mom asked, "Do you want it?"

I immediately replied, "Yes!"

She told me, "I will give it to you under one condition."

I asked, "What is the condition?"

She told me, "I want you to put it on your bed as soon as you get home."

I agreed, and the first of my little miracles manifested right before my eyes.

The first thing I did when I returned home a couple of days later was to put the bedspread on the bed, which made me smile. That bedspread was like receiving a hug from my family each night as I crawled into bed. Yes, I still have the bedspread on my bed. It still makes me smile and will probably be there for quite some time.

I share the bedspread story with you as an example of how you can use the law of attraction to bring things to you. It is a small example, and those not familiar with the law of attraction might call it a coincidence. I know it was not a coincidence that I was dreaming of a beautiful bedspread, but my use of the law of attraction made it happen. I was able to be very clear on what I wanted, I visualized it, and boom, my mom had the perfect bedspread, better than I had imagined. That was not a coincidence but a manifestation in action. Yes, it is a small example, and having the perfect bedspread is not my life's goal, but it was something that I wanted, and I brought it about. We will get into how the law of attraction works shortly, but I thought a simple example would show that anyone can put the practice into play.

The law of attraction is always at work—thoughts become things. So, if I had focused on how awful my life was going to be after the divorce, it would have been.

The process of learning the law of attraction is like learning anything, for example, reading. You start with the basics, like learning the alphabet. You keep practicing, reading, learning, moving from the alphabet to small words, and then putting sentences together. You get the idea. You don't learn to read *Harry Potter* before you learn the alphabet. Same with learning how to use the law of attraction.

When I first started hearing about the law of attraction, I didn't know what it would do for me or where it would take me, but my first exposure was watching the movie *The Secret* and then reading books by Esther and Jerry Hicks, Louise

Hayes, Wayne Dyer, and others. Again, I thought if other people had success using the law of attraction, why couldn't I? I also remember thinking it didn't cost lots of money and I could do the exercises on my own at my convenience without disrupting my life. It felt similar to starting a diet. You don't want to tell everyone in case it doesn't work, but you are hopeful.

Putting the law of attraction into practice has helped me not always jump to the worst-case scenario. It has taught me that by focusing on joy and what makes me happy, the rest of my life becomes much easier to deal with. It is not wrong to put myself first and to do what makes me happy. It has brought me to other like-minded positive people and allowed me to disengage from those negative thinking people who were holding me back. The law of attraction has changed my life for the better.

As one of my friends said, "You seem better, not bitter."

I really wanted to write this to help other people, especially moms, learn to think more positively and begin their journey with the law of attraction. As moms, we give the best to the people in our lives every day and often feel like our cup has a hole in the bottom. We put everyone else first and often feel like we have lost ourselves along the way. Learning and practicing the law of attraction has helped me find me again, and it has taught me how to help my daughter handle those curveballs in life.

We want to protect our children. I think we need to make sure our kids know they are loved, give them situations where they will gain confidence, and teach them to take chances and go for what they want, rather than focusing on being careful and thinking about everything that could go wrong. We also need to help them take ownership of their decisions and realize their mistakes are really opportunities to learn and grow. This book will teach you how to redirect your thoughts, which in turn will help you change what you think and what you say. As parents, we can then teach our kids how to think and redirect their thoughts when bad things happen. We all want the very best for our kids. This book will help you learn how to think positively. Kids learn from what we do. So, let's give them the very best example of a positive approach to life.

I would love to see the law of attraction principles taught to elementary students. What a change we would see in the world if everyone had the knowledge to train their brain to think positively and harness the law of attraction to achieve their dreams instead of living in a negative frame of mind.

I spent a large portion of my career working with salespeople and eventually became one myself. The top salespeople are usually not the best sales coaches or trainers. They get their reward from closing the sales themselves. The best sales trainers, managers, or coaches are those who get their reward from watching those they have trained meeting their sales goals. I am in the second category. I love when my clients have a win and do well. That is my reward. The reason I wrote this book is to be able to help others make their own miracles and manifest their dreams into reality. I am a fairly normal person (most days) and wanted to show people looking for hope a new way of thinking so they can accomplish their dreams and provide simple examples of how the process works. Sometimes we just need a gentle nudge in the right direction. Consider this book your nudge sent with love.

The law of attraction has helped me to really think about what I want, what brings me joy, and to really rediscover myself again. Are you ready for the challenge? Are you ready to reexamine how you think about things and make changes to improve your life? The law of attraction brought you to this point. Invest in you. The return on your investment of time will be amazing!

WHAT IS THE LAW OF ATTRACTION?

"The universe is changing, our life is what our thoughts make it."

—MARCUS AURELIUS

Who doesn't want infinite abundance and joy? For those of you who are just sticking your toes in the water and getting familiar with the law of attraction, in my mind or in a common sense description, it is a way to think. It is a practice to help you reach your goals and live out your dreams. The law of attraction (LOA) is a universal principle that states you will attract into your life whatever you focus on. Whatever you give your energy and attention to is what will come back to you, according to Bob Proctor in his video, "How the Law of Attraction Works." He goes on to state, in his 2015 YouTube video, "The law of attraction allows for infinite possibilities, infinite abundance, and infinite joy. It knows no order of difficulty, and it can change your life in every way if you let it" (Proctor 2015).

It is a very simple concept on paper, but trying to retrain your brain to think in a positive mode and believe you can obtain your wildest dreams can be very difficult, especially if you've had years of negative programming from family, friends, society, and, most importantly, yourself. The great news is you can retrain your brain! You also must take that leap of faith and believe the process works.

As an owner of a small marketing company, I am constantly telling my clients, who are business owners, to be kind to themselves. We all need to work on upping the positive self-talk we have with ourselves every day. Louise L. Hay, a founder in the self-help movement, focused on using positive affirmations to retrain your brain and to be kind to yourself. Louise L. Hay's book *You Can Heal Your Life* was my bible while going through my divorce (Hay 1999, 98-103). The book helped me learn how to allow myself grace and develop new thought patterns. Any form of rejection can be difficult to handle, and this book provided exercises and affirmations, which helped me understand it is not about what happens to me but how I think about and act on what happens. Rejection is the Universe protecting you. I wish I had had this information way back in junior high.

I am a lover of self-help books, but it drives me crazy when an author spends half the book selling me on the concept of whatever the book is about. I obviously know I need whatever the book is about or I wouldn't have bought the book. What I really want is the "how to" and I want it early in the book with details and stories of how "it" works.

My goal for this book is to provide a common sense, no-bullshit perspective on the law of attraction and how you can use it to manifest things you desire while giving you exercises throughout to help you get familiar with the process.

>Total buy-in
>Believe in LOA and want to learn more
>Heard of LOA
>Heard of LOA, curious
>Never heard of LOA
>Non-believer

If you've never heard of the LOA but are open to learning a new way to think and want to improve your life, read on. If you're familiar with the law of attraction, my goal is to move you farther on the scale toward being a believer and understanding it is not something we do just today but more of a continual work in progress, or reprogramming your self-talk and how you think about things. If you're an expert on the law of attraction, many of the exercises will be good refreshers for you, and like anything we learn, it is always good to go back to the basics and review.

Depending on who you listen to or whose book you're reading, the law of attraction can be scientific, spiritual, religious, or a combination of all three. The common sense takeaway is don't get hung up on categorizing what it is but focus on the steps to putting it into practice, which we will get into later in the book. You will also hear interchangeable terms when learning about the law of attraction that include the Universe, the higher power, God, the force, and others. Pick whatever term or terms you like. When we train our brain to think positively, like attracts like and thoughts become things.

> *"Everything in life is vibration."*
> —ALBERT EINSTEIN

The chair you're sitting on has a vibration. You have a vibration. Your surly teenager has a vibration, which can change in an instant. Have you ever been in a meeting or at an event or party where a person comes in and you automatically think, *Oh, this person is sucking the energy out of the room?* If not, you might be that person (just kidding!). That air-sucking person also has a vibration—a low vibration. Now, have you ever met someone whose positive energy is oozing out of their every pore, and they make you feel better about yourself because they are so upbeat? Those two examples are of people on the opposite ends of the vibrational scale.

The lower you are on the vibrational scale, the harder it will be for you to manifest your dreams. Like attracts like. So, if you're miserable or depressed, you're going to bring bad things to you, not good things. Now, if you're that upbeat, positive, happy person, your vibration is much higher, and you will find it easier to manifest your dreams and desires. Below is a vibrational scale of emotions starting with joy and sliding down the scale to fear. Take a few minutes and think about where you are on the scale right this minute. Where do you think you are most days? The goal with the law of attraction is to move yourself up the vibrational and emotional scale so that you can create the life you dream about.

Suzanne Young, author and partner in Personal Success Programs, gave me a laminated card with the Esther and Jerry Hicks Emotional Guidance Scale on it. It is a scale of our feelings and emotions in sequence from our highest vibrational feelings to our lowest. I still carry this card with me and pull it out often to check in with how I am feeling (Hicks and Hicks 2004, 114-115).

When I looked at their scale, I found it interesting there are twenty-two emotions listed with fourteen on the negative side and only eight are on the positive side. I like my scales to be balanced, so I created my own simpler scale using fewer emotions but balanced between good and bad.

1. Joy/Love
2. Peace
3. Excitement
4. Optimistic
5. Content
6. Neutral
7. Irritated
8. Frustrated
9. Despair
10. Hatred
11. Depressed

Where are you on the emotional scale right now? The higher you are on the list, the higher your vibration and the easier it will be for you to attract good things into your life. If you're feeling hatred toward someone or depressed, you're at a low vibration, and it will be much harder to attract good things.

When do you stub your toe, catch your purse handle on the door, or drop or spill stuff? When does your kid choose to throw a hissy fit? This stuff usually happens, in my experience, when I am stressed, mad, or farther down the emotional scale. Like attracts like. After reading this book, you should gain a better understanding of when you're sliding the wrong way on the emotional scale. There will be exercises at the end of the chapters in your Law of Attraction Toolbox for stopping the stinkin' thinkin' and moving up the scale.

I believe you can make the law of attraction as spiritual as you want it to be. I think your spirituality is a very personal thing, and if you're religious you can think of manifesting as praying. For those of you who are agnostic, think of manifesting in more scientific terms. The higher your vibration, the easier it will be to manifest your desires. Use the words you're comfortable with, and don't get hung up on the terms. Focus on the concept and the thought process.

The law of attraction is a universal law. If you're not sure what that means, you're not alone. I didn't know either. According to Study.com, "The concept of universality refers to a precept or principle that is widely accepted as legitimate across locations, time periods, and cultures (Working Scholars 2003). Universal law, then, would be a rule or law that applies in a universal way (Working Scholars 2003)."

Esther Hicks via Abraham Hicks explains that vibrations turn to thoughts. A thought is a vibration, and when you think a thought it gains momentum, and thoughts turn into things (Hicks 2019). My common sense approach then assumes if you're thinking negative thoughts and they gain momentum, those thoughts are headed in the wrong direction. If you're thinking good thoughts, positive thoughts, and they gain momentum, you will continue to have good thoughts. Would you rather watch the boulder roll down the hill or push it up the hill?

Why should you use the law of attraction's thought process? That is a personal, individual answer. For me, it was to bring things into my life I desired and to be a more positive person. It really depends on what you want. Is it more money?

A new relationship? To end a bad relationship? New career? Better health? All the above? It really is up to you.

With the law of attraction comes responsibility. We want to use the law of attraction to bring good things to our lives, but if we focus on the negative thinking, we can also bring bad things to our lives. If the constant message in your head is, "I don't want to get sick, I don't want to get sick," you're focusing on getting sick.

A better message would be to say something along the lines of, "I am healthy, I am healthy." You want your brain and subconscious to focus on healthy, not sick.

I have spoken to many people who believe they are of the positive mindset, but when I listen to how they talk about themselves or to themselves, it is not in a positive light. Really listen and think about how you talk to and about yourself. Do you catch yourself saying things like, "I'm so stupid," or "I can't believe I made that stupid mistake"? I encourage people to use the word "when," not "if," when referring to something they are going to do. Using the word "when" assumes it will happen. Using the word "if" is less positive. That seems like a very small distinction, but saying *when* instead of *if* is assuming the good thing will happen. Definitely more positive than *if* it happens.

According to the article, "Positive Self-Talk: How Talking to Yourself Is a Good Thing" in *Healthline*, "Self-talk can enhance your performance and general well-being" (Holland 2020).

Furthermore, positive self-talk and a more optimistic outlook can have other health benefits, including:

- increased vitality
- greater life satisfaction
- improved immune function

- reduced pain
- better cardiovascular health
- better physical well-being
- reduced risk for death
- less stress and distress

It's not clear why optimists and individuals with more positive self-talk experience these benefits. However, research suggests "people with positive self-talk may have mental skills that allow them to solve problems, think differently, and be more efficient at coping with hardships or challenges. This can reduce the harmful effects of stress and anxiety" (Holland 2020).

A similar example along the topic of finances would be to say, "I have more money than I need" versus "I don't want to be broke." Take a few minutes and rework the examples below to turn them into positive messages for your brain.

Negative Messages	**Positive Messages**
I don't want to get injured.	_____
I want to stop working at dead-end hourly jobs.	_____
I want to stop dating jerks.	_____
I don't want to be fat.	_____

GET YOUR HEAD RIGHT

―――

"Attitude is everything, so pick a good one."

—WAYNE DYER

Think about the last time you had a bad day. Was it one thing that went wrong or a series of events all day? My experience with bad days is that they usually start that way, and the hits keep coming. When you're in the middle of a bad day, it can be difficult to get out of the funk. We say things like, "What else can go wrong today?" which is almost inviting more bad stuff to happen. Remember, like attracts like, good or bad. So, if we are thinking, *This is a bad day*, all day long, we are right via a self-fulfilling prophecy.

Those days it feels like everything and everyone is working against us. Early in the divorce process, I woke up angry and feeling sorry for myself. I didn't do my gratitude journal or read my affirmations that morning. The dog made a mess in the house, the cat had a serious hairball, and I spilled my smoothie down the front of my shirt. This was all before 8:00 a.m. Fortunately, the little LOA lightbulb went off in my brain. I went back to bed, wrote in my gratitude journal, read my affirmations, and had a redo of my morning. The rest of the day was very pleasant.

Both good and bad feelings exist in our heads. It's kind of like the devil and the angel sitting on our shoulders trying to bring us to their side. The good news is we are in charge of our thoughts. The bad news is we are in charge of our thoughts.

Now think of the last time you had a great day. What were you doing? How did you feel? Didn't it feel like you could do anything or accomplish anything? On good days, things seem easy. That is where we want to get to every day. Once you've moved up the vibrational scale, more good things keep happening. The more good things that keep happening, the more good things you can bring to yourself. Before we can manifest our goals and desires, we need to get to a point where we have more good days than bad days.

You have the power before your feet hit the floor in the morning to tell yourself you're going to have a great day. Even if it is a dark dreary day and you're not feeling it, if you start your day with telling yourself you're going to have a great day, you're giving yourself the power to make it so. It doesn't cost you any money, and that positive self-talk will move you up the emotional scale. Truth be told, I often tell the cat and dog we're going to have a great day today. They can't talk back, but I think they get the message

The law of attraction begins with loving yourself. Don't groan. It is true. The law of attraction won't work until you love yourself. If you don't love yourself first, it is hard to love other things or people and for them to love you. When you're not loving yourself, you're talking to yourself in a negative way, which automatically pushes you down the emotional scale (Hicks and Hicks 2004, 114-115). I think most of us are guilty of being unkind to ourselves. Often, I hear people say things like, "I'm so stupid," or "I'm such an idiot."

That self-talk might be said in jest, but your self-conscience doesn't know the difference. Try to talk to yourself as you would to your very best friend for a day. We need to take a lesson from our dogs. Try loving yourself as much as your dog loves you.

Most of us have had some programming from the time we were babies from our family and friends, not all of it positive. My mom has always been supportive, but I can remember coming down the stairs in an outfit I thought looked great and I would hear something like, "You're going to wear that?"

My fashion sense was not always on point, and she was saying it out of concern. I just remembered the negative feeling. I was not thinking my mom had my best interest in mind. My parents always told me I could do whatever I wanted, but our brains remember those negative comments.

In Allie Caren's *Washington Post* article, "Why we often remember the bad better than the good," many studies suggest we are more likely to remember negative experiences over positive experiences, and according to Laura Carstensen, a psychology professor at Stanford University, in general, we tend to *notice* the negative more than the positive (Caren 2018).

I grew up in a loving household, so imagine when a child grows up in an unloving home with negative comments every day. That person is going to have more work to start loving themselves.

Beginning the loving-ourselves process starts with recognizing we have all been programmed and understanding we can't go back in the past and have a do-over. We shouldn't spend time regretting the past because it can't be changed. We need to start with our actions today to begin loving ourselves. Repeating daily affirmations is one way to begin the self-love process.

An affirmation is a positive phrase, statement, or sentence that helps overcome negative thoughts. An effective affirmation is one that makes sense for you, touches you, inspires you, or motivates you. The key is to repeat the affirmation to yourself throughout your day. When you feel yourself becoming negative, depressed, sad, stressed, or scared, repeat your affirmation or affirmations to stop the negative self-talk. You can have and use as many affirmations as you want. Below is a list to get you started or get creative and write your own.

Suggested Affirmations	**Your Personalized Affirmations**
I deserve the best and expect the best.	1. _____
I rock.	2. _____
I love myself.	3. _____
I am a great person.	4. _____
I am smart, sexy, healthy, and fun.	5. _____

Jumpstart the affirmation process by looking at yourself in the mirror and saying your affirmation several times out loud. You will feel funny talking to yourself out loud at first. When you look in the mirror, look deep, deep into your eyes when you say your affirmation. It will become easier. Get in the practice of saying your affirmation throughout the day. If you're in the office, you may want to whisper your affirmation or say it silently when others are around. I also recommend writing the affirmation down on a piece of paper and sticking that in your wallet. Feel free to write the affirmation out daily too. I find when I write my affirmation down, it sticks in my brain better.

"Consider affirmations as a form of positive self-talk that can change your point of view, enhance your mood, and relieve depression symptoms" (Kristenson 2022). Do you know anyone who doesn't want to enhance their mood and relieve depression symptoms, especially with no drugs, illegal or legal? So, just by saying positive things to yourself daily, you can improve your mood. That is amazing to me. It is so simple. Yet, it takes discipline and belief that it works. It doesn't cost anything, and if you're like me, I am talking to myself all day anyway.

How many mornings do you say things to yourself like, "I'm so fat," or "I look so fat, none of my clothes fit," when you're getting dressed.

According to the CDC, the US obesity prevalence was 41.9 percent in 2017-2020 (2021). Negative self-talk about weight is also very popular. Focusing on being fat is telling yourself that you are fat. Likes attract likes, and negative self-talk is a sure-fire way to slide down that emotional scale and up on the pound scale. A better choice for self-talk would be to be thankful for your body and your health. Focusing on your good health and being grateful for everything your body does for you is much better self-talk while you focus on things to help you become healthier.

Paying your bills when you are short on money is not a fun process. I used to dread paying the bills. If you're in a situation where your paycheck doesn't last until the end of the month, try this activity. When you go to pay your bills, instead of thinking, *How can everything be so expensive?* instead, try thinking about how grateful you are for the car you drive as you make your car payment. How having a car allows you to go to work, to see your friends and family, and how truly thankful you are for your car. List out how all the good things the bill you're paying benefits you.

You are redirecting your brain from thinking negatively to thinking positively just by reframing your thoughts. People often talk about how broke they are or how expensive everything is without even realizing it. While filling up your gas tank, are you thankful you have a car or ticked off at the price for a tank of gas? When you're paying your bills, are you grateful for the utilities you have in your home or are you irritated? When we are angry, the Universe feels that negative vibrational energy, and because likes attract like, you'll bring more money hardships to yourself. Part of this is just like trying to break any other bad habit. You must become aware of your self-talk, stop the negativity, and then focus on framing things in a positive manner.

Practice Exercise—Instead of thinking or saying the negative thought on the left, rewrite a statement in a positive way.

Example 1

Negative Statement	Reframed in a Positive Light
I am so broke.	I love having more than enough to pay my bills.
This bill is ridiculous.	Thank you for the service you provide.

I can't believe I gained all this weight.	_____
	_____
My nose is too big.	_____
	_____
My eyes are too close together.	_____
	_____
I have made so many mistakes in my life.	_____
	_____

This is where the work begins, I can tell you to think positively, but if you're depressed or angry, that probably isn't going to be effective. You will need to take some time to sit down and think about what makes you happy. Go outside, sit in the sun, and make a list of 100 things that make you happy. This list could include people, things you do, activities, things you see, food you love, animals, weather, whatever makes you happy. Everyone's list will be different. Once you have this list, take your calendar and plan times to do, see, feel, taste, or smell those things on your list.

Physical activity or movement is another simple way to get your vibrational level up. According to *Harvard Health Publishing*, "Running for 15 minutes a day or walking for an hour reduces the risk of major depression, according to a recent study" (2019).

I like the term "moving" better than exercise. Exercise feels like I should do it, and moving is doing something I enjoy. Moving could be walking your dog outside, a dance party for one, or playing ping pong with your kids—whatever you enjoy that gets your heart beating and gets you moving.

Exercise is the best form of anti-depressant that only has positive side effects like sleeping and feeling better. If you have been a serious couch potato, start slow and work your way up to more time moving. Physical activity is a simple way to help move you up the vibrational scale.

You can't escape the law of attraction even in your darkest moments. The more you focus on how bad things are, the more you bring bad things to you. Two people could have the same thing happen to them. Maybe they both started the day by spilling coffee on themselves in the car on the way to an appointment with a client. The first person is angry, throws a fit, and continues their rant on their way to the appointment. They proceed to tell their client how awful their day is and then doesn't close the sale. The second person isn't thrilled with a coffee stain down the front of the shirt but laughs it off, meets with the client, and makes a joke they need to carry a bib in the car. Guess who closes the sale and has a great day, and guess whose day is a total disaster? It's all in perspective and how we decide to think about things.

If you're not feeling the most joyful, here is an exercise to raise your vibrational level. Get a notebook and a pen and put it on your nightstand. Every morning before you get out of bed, take five minutes and write down ten things you're thankful for. You can get fancy and buy a beautiful journal and a nice pen or take out that leftover spiral notebook from your kid's third-grade English class and whatever writing utensil you can find. The important thing is to write down ten things you're thankful for every day for a month. It can be your dog, your kids, your health, little things, or big things. Whatever it is at that moment, write it down.

We can always find something to be grateful for even when going through the terrible times in our lives. If you're an over-achiever, you can write in your gratitude journal before you go to sleep too. That way you are starting and ending your day with gratitude, which will automatically raise your vibrational level.

Going through my divorce was the most tumultuous ten months of my life. However, I kept a gratitude journal, which helped raise my vibrational level, and even though I was going through a shit show, I had some really great things happen to me. And to be honest, I decided early in the proceedings that I wasn't going to give anyone the power to mess up my day. Following is an excerpt my gratitude journal on 7/23/21:

> *So grateful for:*
> *Rachel*
> *The flooring guys*
> *My realtor*
> *For my new house when I am ready to purchase*
> *My health*
> *My friends*
> *The abundance of wealth I am receiving*
> *The ability to manage my finances*
> *My family*
> *The pets*
> *The sunshine*

During this time, we were in the negotiations of the divorce, which very stressful. By using the LOA, my gratitude journal, and affirmations, I made it through.

Taking responsibility for the way we feel every day is a choice. It is a little scary, too, because as we take responsibility for our feelings and thoughts, there is no one else to blame but ourselves. So, it is empowering and scary at the same time. We can't blame anyone for how we are feeling. People may do things to irritate us or even make us angry, but we are in control of our thoughts and how we react to whatever they said or did. It is easy to blame someone else for how we are feeling, but in reality, we are in control of our thoughts. It really is about taking the responsibility and control of how we react and think about things. I like to tell myself, "I am not going to let anyone mess up my day because of what they said or did." Take control of your thoughts and reactions.

Thoughts become things, so keep practicing positive thinking. It can be difficult to do that at times, especially on those days when everything seems to be working against us. We all stumbled as children, but we didn't stop learning to walk. Eventually, you will be able to recognize when you are thinking negatively, and you'll be able to stop yourself and change the direction of those thoughts. Be kind to yourself and keep going.

Take charge of your thoughts. Be the positive thinking boss who isn't going to let anyone or anything mess up your thoughts. Don't give up that power and control you have over your mind.

WHAT ARE YOUR THOUGHTS ON THE LAW OF ATTRACTION?

"We become what we think about."

—EARL NIGHTINGALE

Have you ever had an idea and were not sure what your family and friends would think about it? Maybe you were even nervous or downright scared to talk to them about the topic? Sometimes it is easier to approach strangers or people you don't know as well because you're not risking as much personally. The law of attraction falls into this category for me.

It has been an interesting process learning within my circle of friends, clients, and business associates what people think about the law of attraction. My business associates tend to be more open to the law of attraction and believe in it. I think because likes attract like, we are drawn to each other by the Universe. Our mindset determines the quality of our day and the experiences we have and the people we meet.

I have had my own marketing company for ten years, helping small businesses and organizations with their efforts either by teaching them how to do things or doing the work for them. With my clients, I tread cautiously on coming out pointblank and asking what they think about the law of attraction. What I do is spoon feed them activities that will get them thinking positively about themselves and their businesses. It is kind of like Jessica Seinfeld's cookbook *Deceptively Delicious* on how to sneak vegetables into your kids' food without them knowing it (Seinfeld 2009). I don't want to turn them off the ideas and tools to learn the law of attraction if they have pre-conceived negative thoughts about it.

When I work with clients, I can quickly determine if they are in a good place or not with their thoughts. For people who are farther down the emotional scale, a revealing place to start is talking about their exercise, eating, and sleeping habits. If they are down in the dumps and are not moving or exercising, that is a good place to start to improve their thoughts. Have you ever gone for a walk and afterward thought, *Gosh, I wish I wouldn't have gone on that walk?* I am betting the answer is no.

"'One in ten adults in the United States struggles with depression, and antidepressant medications are a common way to treat the condition. However, pills aren't the only solution. Research shows that exercise is also an effective treatment. For some people, it works as well as antidepressants, although exercise alone isn't enough for someone with severe depression,' says Dr. Michael Craig Miller, assistant professor of psychiatry at Harvard Medical School" (Harvard Health Publishing 2021).

Most of us know the more we move, the better we feel, but it is the getting started part that is difficult. When I fall off my exercise program and want to motivate myself to get back on track, I will try a new app or get a new pair of tennis shoes or workout clothes to inspire me to get back to the gym or pool. I'll be honest, I play these kinds of games and tricks with myself all the time. I also try not to use the word "exercise," because it feels like it is a chore, and I don't really enjoy doing chores. I think "moving" is a better word for my brain. It sounds happier than exercise. One of my daily goals is to move for at least thirty minutes every day.

I start by asking my clients to write down their goals for the next year, both personal and professional. Usually, they come back with a list of unspecific goals, so their next assignment is to get specific, meaning if they wrote down they want to increase their income, I ask them, "If your income is $1.00 more this year than last year, would that be enough?" Then they get the idea and get more specific. I like for their goals to be achievable but with a stretch. I am a huge proponent for writing goals down. In an article by Marie Forleo, a study done by Dr. Gail Matthews, a psychology professor at Dominican University of California, found that those participants who wrote their goals down daily were 42 percent more likely of achieving them (Forleo 2019). That is huge, people. If you get nothing else from this book, start writing your goals down daily!

After my clients get the lecture about writing their goals down, they come up with their list of specific goals. I ask them to take the time to close their eyes and tell me how it would feel to accomplish all their goals for that year, because we want to get to that feeling, and also so they are visualizing their goals accomplished.

When I ask my friends what they think about the law of attraction, I have gotten answers across the board. Personally, I hadn't heard about the law of attraction until 2006 when the movie *The Secret* came out. That was my first exposure to the law of attraction.

My longtime friends aren't as familiar with the law of attraction. They have heard of it but don't know the specifics and aren't practicing it on a regular basis. They range from very positive people to very realistic, tell-it-like-it-is people. The friends I have made after 2006 tend to be more familiar with the law of attraction. My friends were excited I was writing a book, and after talking to the ones who weren't that familiar with the law of attraction, I asked what they would want to know or why they would pick up my book if someone else had written it.

The clear answer was that they would want to know the specifics on how to make the law of attraction work for them. They want specific things to help them move up the emotional scale, not someone telling them to think positively. Just telling someone to think positively doesn't really help with the how. If you consider yourself a realist or even a pessimist, this book will give you specific activities to improve your position on the emotional scale. Now, you can't do them for a day and then, abracadabra, you're fixed. It took your whole life to get you to where you are right now, so you will need to practice the activities consistently for the best results.

We might need to back it up for those of you who don't know where you are on the emotional scale or for those who aren't sure if they are a realist, pessimist, or an optimist. One suggestion to help you figure out where you are is to ask those people you are closest to who will tell you the truth. It is kind of scary, but it will help you get a feel for where you are starting on your journey. You can move up and down the scale throughout the day. My goal is to help you recognize where you are on the scale and show you ways to move up.

Learning the law of attraction is sort of like learning yoga. When I went to my first yoga class and was instructed to go into a seated forward fold, I started to fold and realized there was absolutely no way I was going to be able to completely fold over my legs. I was practically sitting straight up and really trying hard not to let out a loud groan. I was peeking around the class to see how far everyone else was folded over. The first person I saw was the instructor, who was completely folded over with her head on her legs. The rest of the room was a mix of people like me sitting almost straight up and everything in between. Fortunately, the instructor calmed us down and told us not to worry about what everyone else was doing and just fold as far as we could without causing pain and focus on our breath, which would help us move a little farther. She also said to keep coming to class and we would eventually be able to fold over farther. She was right. Mastering anything new takes practice.

Practicing the law of attraction works the same way. It doesn't matter where your neighbor or spouse is on the emotional scale or how they think. You can only control your thoughts and can only start where you are currently on the emotional scale. Understanding where you are and then using the tools and practicing the activities in the book will help you move up the emotional scale and make it easier to manifest what you want.

As you become more practiced in the law of attraction, you will be able to know when you're heading in the wrong direction with your thoughts. You will be able to use your LOA tools to stop the negative thinking and do a U-turn to head back up the emotional scale. You'll also find yourself stopping before going too far the wrong way.

I had that experience last year when I found out how much I was going to owe the IRS. I slid down the emotional scale in seconds. I was sobbing in my car on the way home from my appointment with my accountant, almost physically ill. I did one of those head shakes the cartoon characters do and had a talk with myself, stopping the pity party before it roared into full swing. I told myself that between me and my CPA, we would figure it out. So rather than going into full-out depression or rage, I stopped the negative self-talk and started the pep-talk for myself. I limited the pity party to the ride home and then went back to work.

By practicing the techniques in the book, you will get to the point that you will recognize when you're not thinking positively. You will also learn how to stop the negative thinking, redirect your thoughts, and start thinking positively. I love when my clients catch themselves when they say something negative and then rephrase the statement positively.

If you're a skeptical person by nature but want to improve your life, you may have to work a little harder than someone who is more open and optimistic by nature. Don't give up or quit before you get started. One great book that has stood the test of time and should be mandatory reading for everyone is Norman Vincent Peal's *The Amazing Results of Positive Thinking*. Peale asks, "Does positive thinking always work?" He answers, "Yes" (Peale 1959, 1-5).

One activity I do before heading to either a networking meeting or even dinner with friends is to think about what I am going to bring to the gathering. Do I want to add something positive to the group or do I want to dump my bucket and tell them everything that is currently going wrong with my life? Now, we all need that friend who you can dump your bucket with, but you don't want to be known as the Negative Nellie in your group. Are you adding positive energy and bringing the energy level of the group up, or are you dragging everyone down?

What's a quick fix to get you in a positive mood before seeing your group? Put on a happy playlist of songs. There are playlists of happy songs already created, so no excuses that you don't have time to put one together. Second, I always write down my intentions if I am heading to a networking group or even dinner with friends. It could be something as simple as wanting to have a night of laughter if I am meeting my friends. If it is a networking group, I try to start with how I am going to help someone and then follow-up with something like, *I want to meet two new clients and meet someone I can collaborate with.* When I take the minute to write down my intentions, it is amazing how often what I write down happens. This is so simple, yet we tend to fight the idea that it could work. So, my skeptics, this is a good exercise for you. You also must take that leap of faith it will work. Here is where people fall off the wagon. They want to dismiss the idea it could work.

Why not give it a chance? What is the worst thing that could happen? You won't be physically hurt. You won't have to tell me or anyone else if it worked or not. And how great will it be when it does work? You'll be able to accomplish bigger and more important things in your life, but you must be open enough to give it a chance and put these little exercises into practice.

To-Do #1

Write down your intentions before you go to your next meeting, dinner, or event.

My intention(s) for the event are

_____

_____

_____

_____

_____

_____

How did you feel after writing down your intentions?

There is no way this will work.
Not sure if this will work or not but will give it a whirl.
It would be hard to believe, but wouldn't it be great if it worked?
I really hope this works.
I know this will work.

How did your intentions compare to your results?

_____

_____

_____

_____

_____

_____

How did you feel about your results?

_____

_____

_____

_____

_____

_____

To-Do #2

Write down your goals for the day. Get in the habit of doing this daily, and see what happens. Make a commitment to yourself.

My goals for today are:

1. _____

2. _____

3. _____

4. _____

5. _____

6. _____

7. _____

COINCIDENCES, SIGNS, AND SYNCHRONICITIES

"Coincidences mean you're on the right path."

—SIMON VAN BOOY

Experiencing coincidences, signs, and synchronicities is the Universe letting you know you are on the right path and to keep going. Think of them like road signs you follow when there is a detour on the highway to let you know you're on the right route.

    Have you ever been thinking about something and then suddenly what you're thinking about presents itself to you in a sign or by something happening? Let me give you an example. I had moved into my new home that desperately needed landscaping. I had been reading, researching, and thinking about how I could use native plants in my yard. I wasn't sure what to do or how to create a flowerbed design. I went to a networking event, and the director of a non-profit pollinator organization ended up sitting next to me. I had heard of her, and she was on my list to call, and she ended up sitting next to me. I told her I was so happy she was sitting next to me and that I wanted to landscape my yard with native plants. From her purse, she whips out a bunch of information about native plants and sample flowerbed designs. That is an example of being at the same vibration, or "tuned in." Coincidences, signs, and synchronicities often arrive when you're wondering if you're doing the right thing and just before something good happens.

We're going to talk about the differences between the three words and how they relate to the law of attraction. So much information is at our fingertips, and everyone claims to be an expert. When researching and looking up the definitions of the three words, people have lots of opinions. I am going to break it down from my perspective and from my experiences learning the law of attraction.

First, let's look at the definitions. These are definitions I liked and made sense to me. Remember, we are approaching this from a common sense perspective to get you a basic understanding and pique your curiosity about the law of attraction. By definition from my 1968 Thorndike Barnhardt dictionary, red cover and all, "A coincidence is exact correspondence; agreement; especially, the chance occurrence of two things at such a time as to seem remarkable, fitting, etc." (Thorndike and Clarence 1968). From Oxford Languages, a coincidence is a remarkable concurrence of events or circumstances without apparent causal connection (Oxford Learner's Dictionaries 2022).

From the common sense perspective, coincidences are smaller things that happen between two people at the same place on the vibrational scale. One example of this would be if you and a coworker show up in the same outfit to work one day. I can't tell you how many times my mom, sister, and I would plan to meet for a weekend, and we would end up in the same or very similar outfits. We all live in different states and didn't coordinate our outfits but would look like we were planning a family picture.

I couldn't find a great definition for the word sign. So here is my definition. A sign in regard to the law of attraction is something that happens or signals that whatever you are trying to manifest is about to happen or that you're on the right track to manifesting your desire. In my experience, the Universe or God was letting me know I was on the right path and know everything would work out the way I wanted or even better. Someone not familiar with the law of attraction would call a sign a coincidence.

Here is an example of a sign I received while going through my divorce. We were in the middle of negotiating our settlement, and things were not pleasant. Keep in mind that we were living under the same roof during the whole process. Not fun, and I certainly don't recommend it to anyone if it can be avoided. But that was my reality. The day before had been particularly tense, but I had read my meditations that night, woke up, read some more meditations, and dragged myself out of bed on a cold Michigan morning to head for a swim at my workout facility. Swimming kept me sane during the whole divorce.

It was about a fifteen-minute drive, and as I started thinking about the divorce stress from the day before, I started to cry. Honestly, I had a brief pity party for myself for about five minutes, sobbing uncontrollably. But I checked myself out of the pity party and told myself that lots of people had gotten divorced and lived to tell the story. I wasn't unique, and I also had lots of advantages that other people didn't have. I had my own business and could make more money if I needed it. I was healthy, and I worked my way through all the good things I had going for me, including an army of friends and family on my side. I could physically feel myself coming out of the pity party and moving my vibrational, emotional level up the scale. Suddenly the dark dreary sky opened, and this beautiful sunrise appeared. I felt a warmth or burst of energy travel from the top of my head to the tip of my toes and out my fingers, and I couldn't quit smiling. Then I started laughing. In the five minutes prior, I was bawling my head off, and now I was smiling, and nothing had changed except my thoughts. I truly believe that sunrise was a gift from the Universe, telling me to hang on and that my life would be better than I could ever imagine.

The term "synchronicity" came into popular use by Swiss psychotherapist Carl Jung. He experienced "meaningful coincidences" where two or more signs that occurred randomly were also connected by meaning (not by cause) in both his life and during sessions with clients (Jung 1960, 21-23). From Merriam-Webster, a synchronicity is a simultaneous occurrence of events that appear significantly related but have no discernible causal connection (Merriam-Webster 2022).

A good example of the law of attraction in action is when I am thinking about someone and how I should give them a call, and suddenly they are calling me. I used to call this a coincidence before I became familiar with the practice of the law of attraction. Now I understand I was in a good place, higher up the vibrational emotional scale, and I was focusing on this person. We were in alignment with each other.

The law of attraction states like attracts like, so if you're focusing on something, thinking about it all the time, writing down what you want and when you want it, and taking action to make it happen, the Universe wants you to have it and will bring it to you.

When you start receiving signs, it means you're on your way to manifesting what you want. You can think about it as a coincidence on steroids or, more accurately, you're moving up the emotional vibrational scale and the law of attraction is starting to work for you. As you really focus on what you want and are taking action, you will receive more signs. These signs can be in the form of numbers, symbols, animals appearing, songs on the radio that have a line in them relating to what you were thinking about, and many other occurrences related to what you are trying to manifest.

As a business owner, I put the law of attraction into practice daily with my clients and for myself. Going through my divorce, I was very worried about my finances. I knew I couldn't focus on what I didn't have, so I put a plan into practice to attract $2,000 more per month. I kept telling myself I was more than capable of making more money and money was easy to come by. I even bought a crystal that is supposed to attract money and put it in my wallet. Well, about halfway through my divorce, I received a call from a client asking if I was interested in a part-time job doing payroll and accounts receivable/payables for their plumbing contractor. *Holy cow, I just manifested more money!* I took the job and worked that and my business for six months until I made it through the divorce. It took the pressure off having to go look for new clients with "divorce brain" and reduced my financial worries for the time being.

What I learned from manifesting that part-time job is that I needed to be more specific on my dreams. While it did relieve the money worries, it was not the job of my dreams.

Sitting in an office, although a nice one, trying to figure out what plumbers meant and read their minds was not joyful for me. The owner of the company was very smart but a man of few words who didn't really want to answer questions, and things became a little tense. He wasn't happy, I wasn't happy, and so I put a new item on my list of things to manifest. This time, I focused on getting new clients for my business who were appreciative, smart, and could afford to pay.

I also took my client list and added five lines for new clients. I labeled those lines New Client #1, New Client #2, and so on. Guess what? Within two weeks of giving my notice to the plumber, I had four new clients that more than replaced the income of the job. My next dream is bigger!

Again, this story is just a simple example of how to make the law of attraction work for you. Now, a key part to making the law of attraction work is that you can't just sit on your rear-end and wait for things to happen. If I had sat in my house waiting for the phone to ring, those new clients would not have come my way. A key part to making the law of attraction work is that you have to do activities to make your dreams come true. Yes, you need to dream and focus on what you want all the time. You need to assume it has already happened and think about how you will feel when your dream comes true, but you have to have an action plan too.

A lack of an action plan is where many dreams don't happen. People are afraid to do the work or think they won't be able to make their dreams come true because of negative self-talk. In the above story where I picked up new clients in a couple of weeks, I had been networking, giving referrals to others, and letting people know what I do for almost ten years. I attend networking events regularly, I matchmake business owners so they can refer business to each other, and

I stay in touch with friends, family, and business acquaintances. I ask lots of questions and, most importantly, I listen for what or who people need in their lives.

I believe if you are open and really focusing on what you want, you will receive signs. You also need to know that what you are receiving is a sign or synchronicity in action and that things will work out and you will be able to live the life you want. The following story of synchronicity happened early in the divorce—another miracle.

That miracle is the dining room table that sits in my kitchen today. I clearly remember the day this little miracle happened. It was Sunday, March 17. My on-his-way to being my ex-husband had just informed me that instead of me living in our house with our daughter until she graduated from high school, I would need to move out. The house we were living in was his, and I owned a condo out-of-state. So, instead of having two years to build my business back up after COVID-19, I was now faced with figuring out how I was going to afford a place to live and pay for everything sooner versus later.

I was sitting in the living room, trying to stay positive and making a mental list of furniture I would need, which included two beds, a couch, living room chairs, and a dining room table and chairs. I loved having people over for dinner, and we would always end up at the kitchen table. As I am making my mental list, I am thinking about what kind of house I wanted, which included a dining area open to the kitchen, so if I was cooking I could still be in on the conversation. In the old house, we had a table that could only seat six comfortably. In my new house, I was visualizing a big table that could seat ten or twelve.

After I finished visualizing my new house's dining room and completing my mental list of furniture I would need, I jumped on Facebook to see if I had any client notifications I needed to address. Keep in mind, we had just begun the divorce process, and I wasn't sure when we would be divorced or when I would be moving out. I also didn't know the size of my future new house or the layout or colors.

The first thing that popped up on Facebook was a woman in the city next to mine giving away what appeared to be an old solid oak table with a large leaf and eight chairs. Giving away! I messaged her and asked, "Can I come over right now and take a look at the dining set?"

She told me, "Yes, and I won't give the set away until you have a chance to look at it."

So, I jumped in my car, thanked God/the Universe for bringing me the table, and drove to her house. The table, leaf, and chairs were solid wood but old and in need of some love.

I asked the woman, "Can I give you some money for the set?"

She told me, "No, and I feel bad getting rid of the set because it was my mom's, but I don't have room for it in my house, and it has been taking up space in my garage. I want it to go to someone who will appreciate the set."

I started to cry and told her, "I am getting divorced, and I will restore the table and chairs and take good care of them."

We both ended up crying, and she gave me a big hug and said, "Everything will work out."

She was right. My next issue at hand was figuring out where I was going to put the table and chairs and how I was going to get them there. I called a client who knew I was going through a divorce and also had a big truck and a commercial building.

After he answered the phone, I asked, "Can you do me a favor?"

He asked, "What's the favor?"

I replied, "Could you pick up an old dining room set and chairs for me?"

He said, "I can tomorrow morning."

I then asked, "Can you store the table and chairs for me for a while?"

He said, "Yes, and I will meet you tomorrow morning to pick up the table and chairs."

The table and chairs were safely stored by my client for five months until I had a rough idea of when I would be moving. I brought the set back to the house I was living in and refinished the table and chairs. This beautiful round oak table will seat ten to twelve with the leaf. I refinished it natural on top and painted the base a slate blue. It took lots of elbow grease and time, but it is beautiful and makes me smile every time I walk through my dining room. Another little miracle I manifested.

I truly believe finding this table a minute after I was visualizing my new house and dining room was not a coincidence but a message from the Universe that everything was going to be okay, and it was.

As you practice the law of attraction and get yourself moving up the emotional scale, the more you will experience coincidences, signs, and synchronicities. This also means you are on the right path toward manifesting your own miracles.

Recognizing and being grateful for coincidences, signs, and synchronicities will bring about more good things for you. Before understanding the law of attraction, I floated through life with good things happening but didn't understand or appreciate their significance. Now when I receive a sign, I will take a moment and say out loud, "Thanks, Universe." Being grateful for those signs makes you happier and will bring about more signs. Stay in the present moment so you can receive and recognize those signs. When you receive a sign, send a little thank you out to the Universe!

HOW TO USE THE LAW OF ATTRACTION—MONEY

"The key to abundance is meeting limited circumstances with unlimited thoughts."

—MARIANNE WILLIAMSON

What if you could have more than enough money to live your dream life by changing how you think? Would you be able to have faith that a process worked if you followed the steps? I believe you can learn to use the law of attraction to live that dream life you have always wanted. By working on self-love and moving yourself up the emotional vibrational scale, you can dream big, focus, and work toward your goal, and the Universe will deliver what you're asking for. The better, happier, and more joyful you become, the easier it will be for the Universe to deliver what you want. As you're moving up the emotional scale, you'll find it easier and easier to manifest your desires. The next several chapters will address common things people desire when putting the law of attraction into practice.

Money is a very common theme people are desiring when using the law of attraction. Have you ever heard anyone say they have too much money? The skeptics might find the idea you can manifest more money hard to believe.

We all have our own set of beliefs, which were created by our own set of circumstances. These circumstances include the early influences in our life, parents, caregivers, siblings, friends, bosses, teachers, mentors, and more. Beliefs are not necessarily factual. How did your family feel about money? How did they talk about money? Did you hear statements like, "You'll never have enough money," or "You have to work hard for everything you earn." We each come with our own unique set of baggage or hang-ups about money from years of programming by our family and friends. Were your friends of the mindset that you need to have an eight-to-five job with a steady paycheck and that you had to put your time in, or were you more comfortable taking risks for the opportunity of a bigger reward? We need to recognize we might have negative programming about money and then, by using daily affirmations about money, work at dismissing those negative thoughts.

Money Exercise #1

Think about the negative messages you received as a child about money. Write those thoughts or sayings below in the left column and then rephrase the message positively in the right column.

Negative Money Statement Examples:

Rich people are bad people.
Money doesn't grow on trees.
You'll never jump more than one economic class than you grew up in.

Negative Money Message   **Positive Money Message**

1. _____   _____

2. _____   _____

3. _____   _____

4. _____   _____

5. _____   _____

I have a friend who thinks I am crazy for running my own business with no guarantee of a steady paycheck and knowing that my clients can leave anytime. I know by running my own business, I can always make more money and have the flexibility to work my schedule to fit my life. I have had an eight-to-five job in the past and always felt like a prisoner waiting for my next break or for lunch, counting the minutes until I could leave. Neither my friend nor I are wrong, but we both know what we want. My friend would never take the risk of starting her own business and has admitted she doesn't have the discipline to work from home running her own company. Again, we all have a set of beliefs and baggage and want different things.

Using the law of attraction is like putting your order in at a restaurant. You ask for what you want. In this example, if it's more money, you focus on that money night and day, and by focusing I mean in a positive way, so you are thinking of the abundance of money, not the lack of money. For example, you don't want to think something like, *I don't want to be broke each month.*

Instead, you want to think, *How great it is that I have a surplus of money every month and have more than enough money?* Think about how wonderful that feeling of having an abundance of an extra $2,000 a month is and then what activities you are doing to bring that money to you. Sitting on the couch and just hoping isn't going to cut it. Maybe you start a side gig or pull some overtime or sell the junk in your basement. The key is to focus on your goal and do things that will create more money and be open to new opportunities to make more money.

I have seen this process work time and time again in my marketing business. I work with my clients to have them get specific on their money goals. Then we work on a marketing campaign for new business with consistent marketing efforts. What happens is that all of a sudden, they start getting new clients. Thoughts become things. The new clients might not be from the campaign they are running, but because they are running a consistent campaign with focused positive goals, they are using the law of attraction and manifesting new clients. The key is that my clients are focusing on what they want, have worked hard toward their goal, and have put consistent, ongoing efforts to reaching their goals. If they had only written their goal down and not worked at a consistent marketing campaign, they wouldn't have met their money goals. Positive thoughts plus targeted consistent action equals results.

I experienced this going through my divorce. I was worried about how I would handle the financial obligations of running and paying for a household by myself. Instead of panicking, I kept telling myself I could make more money and spoke to my current client base so they knew I was going through a divorce. One of my clients was very concerned and asked if I needed anything. He asked if I had an attorney and how he could help me.

He told me the owner of the staffing company he used had a position available that I was qualified for and that he had given the owner my name and number. I spoke with the staffing company owner about the open position. It wasn't a good fit for me but I ended up getting him as a client taking care of the social media platforms for his staffing company.

Napoleon Hill tells the story in *Think and Grow Rich* of how Edward C. Barnes came to work with Thomas Edison. Barnes had a definite goal of working *with* Edison, not for him. The story talks about how Barnes was so clear in his goal and didn't let the fact he didn't know Edison at the time or have the money for the train ticket to get to Edison deter him from his goal. He stayed focused and open to opportunities to get him closer to that goal (Hill 1960, 19-22).

By focusing on what he wanted, Barnes was able to eventually get a meeting with Thomas Edison. During the first meeting, Barnes did not reach the goal of working with Edison in the way that he had imagined. Yet, he didn't give up and eventually worked with Edison. He accepted the initial opportunity of working for him for a small wage as an employee. Barnes stayed focused on his goal of working *with* Edison as a business associate rather than as an employee. The opportunity to work with Edison did eventually present itself, but not how Barnes had imagined.

That is an important lesson to remember about the law of attraction. Staying focused on what you want will often allow the Universe to present you the opportunity to reach your goal, but maybe in a different way than you had imagined. The key is to be open to opportunities that can help you get to your desired goal. People can get hung up on wanting to know when and how they are going to happen. Keep thinking about what you want, framed in a positive way, and don't worry about the how. Know the Universe has more than enough resources and will deliver what you're focusing on. In Mr. Hill's story of Edward Barnes and Thomas Edison, Edison had invented the dictating machine, and his current salesmen were not excited about selling the machine. Barnes knew he could and let Mr. Edison know he could sell it. He was so successful selling it that Edison gave him a national contract, and he made himself rich selling the dictating machine. His thoughts became things (Hill 1960, 19-22).

There are several items to be aware of when attracting more money. First, we want to focus on abundance and wealth, not on being broke or not having enough money. Use your money affirmations daily and set lofty but reachable goals. When you hit those goals, set new goals.

Money Exercise #2

Use the space below to write down each company or person you pay each month. Include your rent or mortgage, car, utilities, credit cards, loans, and so on. In the next column write the total balance due, and in the third column write down the monthly payment. This exercise is a reality check and will help you focus on how to get things paid off.

Who I Pay	Total Balance	Monthly Payment	Target Payoff Date

Once you know where you are right now, you can start focusing on where you want to be and when. As you pay off a debt, that payment can be rolled into the next earliest payoff date. Each month as you update your form, you will see the balances coming down. Get excited about that. If you get a bonus or extra money, apply that to one of your monthly payments. You now know where you are with what you owe and to whom. The next step is to figure out where you want to be and when.

I find it helpful when I am manifesting money to focus on shorter time frames initially so I can get some wins under my belt. For example, I have had goals and manifested smaller amounts by saying I will obtain three new clients in the next month that will generate $1,000 additional income. This helps rather than saying I will increase my annual income by $12,000. I start with one month. Once that happens, I can increase that amount to $2,000 for the next month. That way, my end of the year increase is higher, and I move myself up the emotional scale all year by setting and achieving those monthly goals or targets. If you're working a job where you have a salary and don't have an opportunity to increase your income regularly, you will need to think of additional ways you can make money outside of your job. Do some research and think about what you love to do. Maybe there is a side business you could do that is related to a hobby or activity you are passionate about. The more I speak with people, the more I realize many more people have side gigs than when I was younger. Those side hustles often help people to transition into their dream job or business.

Everyone's financial situation is unique, so first we need to figure out where we are. Second, we need to set financial goals, which will depend on your particular situation. Third, we need to focus on keeping our vibrational and emotional level high. Attracting more money in our life is hard if we are constantly thinking about how broke we are. Third, we need to put an action plan in place to improve our situation. Here is where the thoughts become actions and actions become things. If you just wish your situation improves but have no action plan, no one is going to ring your doorbell and deliver free money. Focused positive thoughts plus an action plan with targeted activity will get you to your desired goal.

If money is something you would like to manifest, how much money do you want? Be specific with how much and when. One note here is that to increase your income, especially when you're getting started with the law of attraction, you want to make a jump in your income in an amount your brain can process. If you want to go from $20,000 a year to $5,000,000 a year, that might be too big of a jump for your brain to believe. So, make a jump that is big but believable so your brain can process it. Once you make that jump, the next jump will be easier to process, and you can keep increasing the amount as you reach that goal and then dream your next goal. The Universe is abundant and can deliver what you ask for.

When I am feeling like I don't have enough money, I stop the negative self-talk immediately. I try and help someone without the expectation of anything in return. There is always someone worse off than we are. By helping someone in that situation, I truly believe the Universe knows, and good things will come back to me at some point. I have donated my time consulting non-profits, and I also like to help younger people just starting their businesses by introducing them to potential referral partners or taking them to lunch and giving free advice. Telling someone there will be no charge other than to recommend me to their friends and business associates if the opportunity arises is fun.

In the last chapter, we spoke about the power of affirmations in helping you achieve your dreams. Affirmations are also especially helpful when trying to manifest more wealth. Below are some money affirmation suggestions. Again, feel free to come up with your own, and say them often!

- I am a money magnet.
- I love money. Money is good.
- I love watching my bank account grow.
- It is so much fun to be able to buy whatever I want.
- I have more money than I need each month.
- I love giving away money because I can always make more.
- I am attracting more money each day.
- I have all the wealth I deserve.
- There is no limit to how much money I can attract.
- I value money and am attracting more and more of it into my life.

- Earning money is easy peasey.
- I am successful in attracting wealth and in achieving all my goals.
- I live a successful, abundant, joyful life.

Attracting more income to you is more than possible. You can improve your financial situation by reframing your thoughts from the perspective of abundance rather than from a lack of wealth. Be specific on what you want in regard to income and make it a number realistic enough your brain can make the jump from where you are to where you want to be. The great thing is once you reach your initial goal, you can set a higher, bigger, better goal.

HOW TO USE THE LAW OF ATTRACTION— CAREER

―

"If opportunity doesn't knock, build a door."

—MILTON BERLE

Most of us have had a job we haven't loved or a job we originally liked that changed because of a variety of possible factors. There are four basic scenarios about how we feel about our current job/business:

1. We don't have a job, and we want one.
2. We have a job, and we don't like the job more days than not.
3. We have a job and like it more often than not.
4. We don't have a job, and we don't want one.

We're not going to worry about the people who don't have a job and don't want one. Hopefully, they are living their best life!

Let's get into the other three scenarios and how and what we need to do to put the law of attraction into play. Remember that the law of attraction is always at work whether you're thinking positively or negatively. Being in a situation where you don't have a job and really want one is not a fun place to be. Your self-talk is really, really important during the job search journey. This is truly a crappy place to be. We tend to tie our identity with what we do. I think men especially have a hard time when they don't have a job and want one. Their identity is more wrapped up in what they do than women. I think women have more interests and friends and are better at reinventing themselves. (Sorry, guys.) Anyway, this is not a place people wish to be. The two times in my career where I found myself without a job when I needed one were very stressful, and my ego was in the dumpster.

Looking for a job isn't physically demanding, but it can be very mentally challenging. Give yourself permission to acknowledge your feelings. Create some kind of routine. Maybe you spend the morning looking for a job, sending résumés, or making calls. Then give yourself time for activities that will keep your mind occupied on something other than looking for a job. Go volunteer at a food bank or babysit for your neighbor's toddler. Nothing is better than hearing a small child laugh. Take your dog for a walk or whatever you enjoy doing that will give your brain a break from thinking about the lack of having a job. I like to bake. I have to pay attention, I feel like I created something, and it makes the house smell good. Cleaning is another good activity. You will feel better with a clean house, and you can take some frustration out scrubbing the bathtub.

I would also find I was often very tired. The mental stress of not having a job would wear me out. If you feel the need for a nap in the middle of the day, be kind to yourself, take the nap, and enjoy it. Then, the next morning, get up and hit the job search activities again. You can't spend twenty-four hours a day every day looking for a job. Taking a break will make you more productive when you hit the job search platforms again.

I struggled with this situation before I started my business and throughout the process of growing my business. I had a successful corporate career and then found myself unemployed. It was very easy to get discouraged. You start to wonder if you will ever get hired, and that self-doubt is very destructive. I had a permanent pit in my stomach through the job search. The second time I found myself in this situation, I ended up starting my business because I didn't think I was going to get hired anywhere. This happened as I was just beginning to hear about the law of attraction, and I didn't do a good job of keeping a positive mental attitude. I feel your pain, but now I know if you put the law of attraction into practice, you will have a much easier time finding a new job.

This is where you really need to put on your positive pants. So back to keeping our heads thinking right. By this, I mean self-talk needs to be positive. Find several affirmations related to jobs and careers that resonate with you, and when you feel yourself starting the negative self-talk, block it by saying your chosen affirmations out loud and often. Now, if you're in the middle of Sunday church service, it is probably better to say those affirmations silently, but keep up the positive self-talk. Write them down too. I know when I am trying to learn something, writing it down helps it stick in my brain. Give it a try and write those affirmations down as you're saying them

Below is a list of career and job affirmations to get you started. If you're not feeling super creative, pick a couple of the affirmations below. Otherwise, write your own and say them often.

"I am bringing my perfect job to me."
"I am the best job hunter in the whole world."
"The Universe is delivering me my dream job."
"I love working with my new coworkers."
"I am a magnet for my perfect job."
"I am ready for the job that will make me feel happy and fulfilled."
"I am uniquely qualified for my new dream job."
"I will work for a company that appreciates my skill set and pays me well."
"I am paid well, happy, and enjoying an abundant life working at my new company."
"I rock it at my new company."

Next, you need to be clear on the type of job you want. What do you love to do? Write down all the things you desire in your new job, which would include the job title, the company or companies you would like to work for, what type of people you'll be working with, what your job will entail daily, benefits, vacation, and work schedule. Write down every little detail. Visualize yourself getting ready in the morning to go to your new job and how it will make you feel to be working at the new company. Know that you are worthy and qualified. Also, use job and career related affirmations to help keep you thinking positively during your search. The better you can see and feel what it will be like in your new position, the easier it will be for you to manifest your new job.

Since this is a more difficult situation to be in and keep a positive mindset, make sure to keep writing in your gratitude journal morning and night. It will help you start and end your day with the right mindset as you work through your job search. If you're someone who doesn't like to write, you are more of a visual person, or the affirmations aren't feeling right, try creating a vision board.

A vision board is a collage of pictures, images, and words that depict your wishes, dreams, and goals to motivate and inspire you daily. You can create a low tech or high tech vision board. For a low tech board, you will need poster or foam board, pictures, words of things that represent your goals and dreams, glue, and scissors. You can pull images from your computer or use old magazines and books. Make a collage of your dreams. Once finished, hang your vision board somewhere you can see it every day. You'll be amazed at what will happen if you keep a positive mindset and think about your dreams visually.

You can also create a vision board using an app to create a collage of your dreams and goals. Canva.com is a free app that is a graphic design platform for those of us who aren't graphic designers. Picmonkey.com is another app where you can create a collage of your goals. Once you create your collage, get it printed and hang it where you will see often. Whether low-tech or high-tech, a vision board is another tool to help you think about and visualize what you want.

Just as a reminder, we must then do the activities that will help us land that perfect job. We can't sit on the couch and hope someone will call us out of the blue. We need to apply for jobs, talk to our contacts, friends, and family, and let them know we're in the market for whatever type of job we want. The saying is true—it's not what you know but who you know. Think of your friends and family as reinforcements and your salespeople to help you find that dream job. Consistent job-hunting activity and a positive mindset will allow you to make the law of attraction work for you.

The next scenario is when you have a job but don't like it more days than you do. This situation isn't ideal, either, so there are some activities you can do to help keep your emotional scale on the positive side and moving up. The difficulty on this step could depend on the reasons why you don't like the job. I have been in this situation too. I found it to be very draining to get up and get ready to go to a job I hated. I finally realized I don't make a good employee and would be much better off working for myself and spending my time looking for new clients instead of looking for a job. Having a job where I had to report to an office every day always felt like I was in prison. I would count the minutes to lunch and closing time. That is no way to live. Maybe the hours aren't good, but you don't mind the work. That might not be as stressful as if you hate your boss or your boss hates you. The exercises will be the same as above, but it is easier to find a job when you have a job and you don't have that panic that you do when you don't have a one. Having no money and no job compounds the stress level more than just having a job you don't like. It can also be very difficult when you have a job you hate but you need to pull the grateful card out and be thankful that you have a job and are getting a paycheck.

Be thankful for your current job, even if it isn't ideal. You could write something like *I am grateful for my experience at XYZ company so that I can appreciate my next job even more.* Being grateful instantly raises your emotional and vibrational level so you will be open to receiving your new job. Also, write down your intention, such as *I am delighted to know that the Universe is bringing me my dream job.* This way, you're assuming your job is on its way, and the Universe delivers what you ask for. You want to say what you're asking for in positive language. Instead of saying, "I want to quit this lousy job so I can find a different job," try saying something like, "I will have my dream job within thirty days, make 25 percent more than I am making now, and will be appreciated by my boss, customers and coworkers."

When we're not happy with our current job or don't have a job, it is easy to let it encompass our thoughts all day and night. Taking care of your health is especially important while in the process of looking for a job. So, keep up your exercise program or start one. Instead of calling it an exercise program, maybe it is "a moving more" program. Choose something that makes you happy. Throw a private dance party and put on your favorite dance songs. It is hard to dance and be in a bad mood. This sounds crazy, but I will also skip when I am feeling down in the dumps. Again, as a grown adult woman, it is hard not to smile when you are skipping. Find those movement activities you love and can't help but put yourself in a better frame of mind. Eating healthy and sleeping is also important, especially during stressful periods in our life.

Know that you will get the job.

The third scenario in regard to finding a new job is when you have a one you like most days, but you are looking for a better opportunity. This scenario is not as stressful as the previous ones. Leaving a job that you like for a better opportunity is a more pleasant way to live and is much easier on your joy level. It is also always easier to find a job when you have a job.

You will want to spend some time thinking about and writing down what your perfect job will look like. Think about what you love to do and what you do well. Hopefully, these two things are in alignment—they usually are. Get specific. Business owners can also use these techniques for attracting new customers, raising their revenue, or even improving their clientele. Next, know that you will find something better. Your power of persuasion over yourself comes into play here. Figure out what your dream job is or, if you're starting a business, what your business would be. See yourself in the dream job, getting dressed in the morning, driving to work, going to the office or place of business, and meeting your new boss or clients.

I did this early as a business owner. For the most part, my clients are wonderful. Early in my career, probably because I was desperate for business, I found myself with a really difficult client who was a true pain in the ass. She was very demanding, not respectful of my time, and not appreciative in any sense. She required a ton of hand holding and wouldn't listen to any recommendations and then argued about my invoice and, in the end, stiffed me for several days' work. Initially I was angry, but I shifted that anger to thinking about the lessons I had learned. This led me to changing some of my processes so I can now recognize potential difficult clients and decline working with them up front.

During the period early in my business when I was dealing with this difficult client, I had been introduced to the law of attraction through a person I met in a networking group. She had given a talk about writing down what you want and putting it out in the Universe. I was skeptical at first but thought, *What could it hurt?* I sat down and wrote out a list of qualities I wanted my ideal clients to possess. I was very specific, and the list was long. Some of the items on the list were that I wanted to work with smart, appreciative, positive people who paid their bills on time, had a sense of humor, were collaborative… You get the idea. Since I took the time to write that list, I have not had any clients not pay their bills, and my clients are all smart, appreciative, and a joy to work with in their own unique ways.

Fulfilling your goals and dreams of a career you love using the law of attraction is definitely possible. It will require more focus and practice if you're in the two situations of having a job you hate or being unemployed. In either of those two scenarios, it is easy to find yourself slipping down the emotional scale and not staying in the most positive frame of mind. The law of attraction is always working. Thoughts become things, so stick with those positive thoughts and be specific about what you want.

HOW TO USE THE LAW OF ATTRACTION— RELATIONSHIPS

―

"Ask for what you want and be prepared to get it."

—MAYA ANGELOU

What would you be willing to do to find the love of your life? People spend lots of time and money on online dating services, which, based on my brief experience, is both time consuming and an interesting study of human behavior. Sometimes hysterical and sometimes scary.

If you're with the love of your life now, congratulations. You probably used the law of attraction and maybe didn't even know it. If you're not with the love of your life, there is hope. The law of attraction can help you to open up and get ready to receive love.

We all have our own set of baggage from our childhood and from our past relationships. We need to really be kind to ourselves when we reflect on our past relationships that didn't work. Rather than beating yourself up for how stupid you were to ignore the warning signs, redirect your thoughts and be thankful for the lessons you learned and won't repeat. Focus on what you want from your next relationship, not what you don't want. An example would be wanting someone who is faithful rather than not wanting to be with a cheater.

"Even if it's been years, or close to a decade since the end of your past relationship, it can have a lasting impact on your life," notes Paulette Sherman, PsyD, psychologist, director of My Dating and Relationship School and author of *Dating from the Inside Out*. "These relationships can impede our current or future relationships or further them, depending on how we have processed them. This is helpful to recognize because our past can either be fodder for our growth or the very thing that holds us back (Sinrich 2020), but if we have not learned from past relationships, they can translate into limiting beliefs and baggage and wounds that will adversely affect us in love," she says.

I am by no means an expert in relationships, but after going through my divorce, something I read really made sense to me. Instead of wishing a certain relationship had never happened, think about what the purpose of that relationship was. What was the lesson I was supposed to or needed to learn? That helped me process some things. The purpose of my marriage was so that my daughter could be born. People get in trouble when they don't learn from past relationships and make the same choices with the same bad results.

Going through a breakup, whether it was a marriage, a long-term partnership, or even a short-term relationship, is not fun and can be emotionally, mentally, and even physically challenging. I remember thinking that pit in my stomach was never going to go away and felt like I was holding my breath for nine months. I know during my divorce, the roller coaster of different feelings came in like waves at the beach. Sometimes it was waves of worry and apprehension. Sometimes it was waves of strength and power. Suddenly finding yourself single can be both terrifying and exhilarating. I was initially really worried about how I was going to handle the financial aspects of being single. The other part of me felt empowered and really excited about my future. My future is now in my hands and my responsibility. I guess it always was, but it feels differently on my own.

Being single, I don't have to compromise with anyone. If I am not happy or not doing something I want to do, there is no excuse. I am in charge. That can be scary if you have been involved with someone for a long time and have had to make compromises to try and make the relationship work. Looking back, I think I made too many compromises on what I was really thinking and feeling to keep the peace. I should have spoken my mind. My ex wasn't a mind-reader. I felt like I needed to put my feelings aside to keep the peace, which is not a great long-term strategy.

While we are talking about self-love, I think it is important to think about the relationship that ended and process all those feelings. Processing feelings and living in the past are two entirely separate things. I knew I had to release the anger I felt toward my ex. After I knew we were getting divorced, I got really mad about all of the stupid things I put up with to keep the peace and felt ticked at myself and even embarrassed by what I didn't speak up about because of the fear the marriage would be in jeopardy.

I must put in a little reminder here that the law of attraction is always at work, whether we are thinking about good things or bad things. Looking back, I can remember an argument my spouse and I had when our daughter was a baby. I don't remember what the fight was about, but I do remember he said something like, "Maybe this was a mistake," meaning the relationship.

That bad thought spoken in the heat of the moment was stuck in my brain, and looking back, I think from that point on my internal dialogue was always thinking, *Is this worth bringing up or should I just let it go to keep the peace?* Ladies, I think we—or I know I—am guilty of remembering all those unkind words. Well, after seventeen years of that, the little things became big things, and there was just too much of thinking the wrong thing. Instead of thinking I need to just put up with this so we don't get divorced, I should have been thinking that I needed to talk to him so that our marriage would stay strong. The thoughts we have become things, so I really, really try and think about what I want, not what I don't want.

We don't want our past relationships to hang us up in our future relationships. I think it is important to spend some time figuring out what I want in a new relationship and thinking about the lessons I learned in the old one. I worry about people who get out of one relationship and jump right into a serious new relationship immediately. For me, it was important to take that time for myself and, more importantly, to focus on my daughter. She was a junior in high school, and before I know it, she will be away at college, so time with her is precious and comes first. The girl is wise beyond her years.

I had asked, "How will you feel when and if your dad and I start dating other people?"

Not to brag, but the girl is brilliant. She said, "I want you both to be happy and meet someone, but I don't need to meet the people you date until it becomes serious and also don't want to meet them if it is a stressful time for me at school."

This helped me think about what I really wanted in a relationship. I want to meet someone who understands my daughter is my priority and that when she is with me, she is and always will be the priority. On the weeks she isn't with me I will have time to spend with someone, and when she goes to college I will have more time. The guys who are looking for the one and need all of my attention now aren't going to be who I spend time with. My thoughts will become things, so I know that Mr. Right is out there and will show up when the timing is right and I am ready.

Now, I am not saying you shouldn't date or stick your toes in the water. I just think it is important to take the time to digest and process the previous relationship before jumping into another serious one. Right now, I wholly endorse casual relationships! As a sixty-year-old woman, there is something very empowering about being able to say to someone that I like you, but I only want something casual right now. Here is when I am free. If that works with your schedule, great. If not, next.

When I was going through my breakup, I can remember thinking, *What if I am never with someone else again?* That made me sad, so I stopped thinking that way. My girlfriend, who has never been married but has had several long-term relationships, told me we were going to go out to a local bar to listen to live music. I didn't have a good excuse not to go, so I reluctantly went along. My thoughts at the time were that I just wanted to have fun and find as much joy as I could every day. Keep in mind, I hadn't been out as a single person for over twenty-four years. The dating world had changed drastically in that time. The pandemic was just a cherry on top of that unfortunate cake. We went dancing, and a much younger man asked me to dance. Talk about great for the ego.

But the self-doubt talk started again. Why would a younger guy want to be with me? So, Miss Common Sense had to know and asked him. He answered, "Older women know what they want and don't play games."

That was empowering in that I can and do express what I want, and if that doesn't work for the other person, I will find someone it does work for.

He also said, "You seem like you have your shit together, and you are fun." The younger man and I know we aren't going to end up together, but for the time being, we have a casual, fun relationship based on friendship. Mr. Right will come along when I am ready. I truly can feel that. It was like my house story in that I knew I would find the right house when the timing was right. The Universe delivers. If we keep thinking about what we want, those feelings become things.

Having gone through a divorce, there were definitely thoughts of *What is wrong with me?* or *Why wouldn't that person love me?* I don't like thinking like that. I liked being mad versus being sad. Being mad gets me fired up to do things for me to prove someone wrong. Apparently, I am motivated by someone doubting me. My dear friend gave me a sign that says, *Underestimate me, that will be fun.*

So, when I felt the self-doubt talk happening in the morning, I would go swim laps. It made me feel better physically and emotionally. I felt good that I was doing something purely for myself. It also gave me time to think about my day and all the things I was grateful for.

I know I am a good person, and I am not going to let anyone make me feel otherwise. This can be hard to do. We need to acknowledge our feelings, but we cannot wallow in a self-pity party. When I am feeling that way, I give myself a time limit and then tell myself I must straighten up and turn my thoughts around. Often, thinking negatively makes me tired, and I will give myself permission to take a nap. Before I fall asleep, I tell myself I will awake with a new attitude and better thoughts. Naps are glorious, and I do wake up feeling better. I change my thoughts so that I am moving up the emotional scale. We can't control what other people think or feel. We really have to focus on our thoughts only.

We must spend the time and do the work so that our relationship with ourselves is a good one. A breakup can be brutal to our self-esteem if we let it. In most breakups, two parties were at fault. Accept your part in the disintegration of the relationship, but don't beat yourself up. I believe a breakup is the opening for better things to come. Move on, and focus on what you do want. Savor the fact the world is wide open, and the love of your life is yours when you are ready.

While going through a breakup or even after a breakup, self-affirmations are once again a good thing to practice. Below are some affirmations to help you get ready for your next relationship.

1. I am lovable.
2. I am open and ready to meet the love of my life.
3. I am ready for head-over-heels love.
4. My past relationships have gotten me ready for the love of my life.
5. I am in the best relationship.
6. My love is passionate, fun, smart, and caring.
7. I am in a relationship with someone who treats me as I want and deserve to be treated.

8. I deserve and expect the best relationship.
9. I am manifesting the love of my life.
10. I love me.
11. I am surrounded by love.
12. I only have heathy relationships.
13. Love starts with loving me.
14. I connect with others easily.
15. I am grateful for all my loving relationships.
16. I attract love.
17. I rock relationships.
18. I am love and light.
19. All my relationships are healthy, loving, and fulfilling.
20. The Universe wants me to be happy and will deliver a loving relationship.

Feel free to make up your own affirmations. Say them often, think them often, and write them down. If affirmations aren't feeling right for you, try the vision board for your relationship. Use words to describe the type of person you want to attract. Think of characteristics that are important to you and put those on a vision board. For the more artistic people, you can also draw your visions too. Be specific on what you're looking for to make it easier for the Universe to deliver your love to you. Focus on what you want, not what you don't want. That is really, really important.

You also have to do some work. Work on loving yourself so that someone else can love you too. Determine what is important to you in a relationship, and get ready to accept that love. I try and take the pressure off and think I want to meet interesting people who will eventually lead into something more serious. Put yourself out there. Say yes to invites from friends, go do things by yourself. Have fun. Happy people attract happy people. I believe the love of my life will appear when I am ready. Stay positive, love yourself, be open, and before you know it, that relationship you've always dreamed about will happen. Are you ready?

THE LAW OF ATTRACTION AND DISEASE

"It is health that is the real wealth, and not pieces of gold and silver."

—MAHATMA GANDHI

What if you could improve or even rid your body of a disease? Would you want to learn more? I believe by thinking positively along with your treatment program, you can improve your results and help with recovery.

Johns Hopkins expert Lisa R. Yanek, MPH, and her colleagues found that people with a family history of heart disease who also had a positive outlook were one-third less likely to have a heart attack or other cardiovascular event within five to twenty-five years than those with a more negative outlook (2021). Being one-third less likely to have a heart attack or cardiovascular event by having a positive outlook? In my book, that is huge! There is no cost, other than your time and focus on thinking positively.

Numerous studies support the notion that positive thinking is good for your health in a variety of ways. One such study found negative thinking signals the body's immune response. A positive attitude can improve your immune system. In an article by Lisa Woods, published in *The Startup*, a meta-analysis of more than three hundred studies covering thirty years of inquiry into the relationship between stress and the immune system found that stressful events can change immune system functioning. The type and duration of stress determines the type of change that occurs (Woods 2019).

Again, I find this great news that when we change how we think, we can affect our health and happiness. That means not blaming others for our negative mood but taking charge of our thoughts and reframing those negative thoughts as soon as we think one can have long-term benefits on our health.

When someone has a disease, there are a multitude of options on treatment, doctors, and more. First, feel good about your healthcare team, and don't be afraid to get a second opinion. Bedside manner makes a difference. If you're not feeling well and your doctor is an ass, how will that make you feel during your treatment and recovery?

Having a disease is like living on a rollercoaster. My cousin had some great advice for my ex-husband and me when we were married. He had a rare kind of melanoma cancer. It took three surgeries to get it out of his body and three surgeries to put his face back together.

She said, "Don't get too down with bad news, and don't get too excited about the good news. Try and keep things as level as possible."

Other advice I have received on dealing with a disease is to not call the disease what it is. For example, don't say the word cancer and give it the power to enter your brain with negative thoughts. Make up a word or call it something that makes you happy. Instead of thinking of unhealthy cells in your body, picture good healthy cells.

Keep negative people and influences out of your world while dealing with disease. Frankly, this is a good thing to do all the time, but especially while going through treatment and recovery. If you live in a metropolitan area, don't watch the local news. It is awful, and I think the news agencies are trying to poison our brains. If I feel the need to know what is happening in the world, I try to just watch the world news every couple of days. If I am feeling down or anxious, I will skip the news and find a funny show or movie that makes me laugh. Ask your friends and family to send you funny memes or jokes to help with the daily laughs.

Once again, the process for using the law of attraction is the same whether we are dealing with our health, relationships, or money. The first step is to ask for what you want, framed positively. When you're asking for what you want, another tip is to ask for the item and then say, "Or better," after. This way, you're signaling the Universe that better works too. Then get ready for the Universe to deliver. Focus on what you want. Then you must have faith the Universe will deliver. This is the step I really need to focus on. I use all my senses and imagine how it will feel, look, taste, and smell to get the thing I am asking for. If you're dealing with a disease, imagine yourself in the healthiest condition of your life and what you will be doing as that happens. Maybe you're running on the beach chasing your kids in the sunshine. Or maybe you're sitting on your deck enjoying the autumn weather in front of a fire. Make it mean something to you and think about how that feels. It should make you smile, which will improve your vibration and move you up the scale.

In Abraham Hicks's YouTube video, "Do This Every Morning for Seventeen Seconds Powerful Manifestation Tool," Esther and Abraham Hicks deliver the message that the most important thing you can do to keep your emotions and thoughts positive is to start your first seventeen seconds of the day with positive thoughts. If you can hold a good thought for seventeen seconds, it will turn into another good thought, and then another. So, before you start worrying about what you have to get done that day, focus on thinking a good thought for seventeen seconds. If you're dealing with a disease, take the first seventeen seconds of your day and think about how you feel with your body in a healthy state. Also, according to Abraham and Esther Hicks, "When you can hold a thought for sixty-eight seconds, manifestation begins" (Hicks and Hicks 2020).

Use your senses and focus on great health. This will take practice and more practice. Don't get discouraged, and if you feel a negative thought sneaking in, reset the clock and turn it into a positive thought. As with most things, the more we practice, the better we get at something. Before you know it, you'll hit the sixty-eight-second mark and beyond, bringing you closer to your desired state of health.

MANIFESTING THINGS

―――

"We receive exactly what we expect to receive."

—JOHN HOLLAND

Good news! The more you put the little exercises into practice, the easier it is to manifest things you want and desire. As I was getting divorced and looking for my new house, I started making a list of things I would need for the house with the idea of manifesting or bringing those things to me. I asked for what I wanted, the Universe answered, and then I allowed it to happen. I wasn't worried about how the things on my list would appear. I had faith they would, somehow or another.

The list was long and ever expanding. When something on my list would appear, I would cross it off and add something else. That is the beauty of the law of attraction. You ask, and the Universe is infinitely abundant and answers. For the skeptics, I was in your shoes initially, but I have a series of "things" stories where I was able to stay positive and focus on what I wanted, and my thoughts became things.

The first step is to make a list of things you want. For the people just getting started in the law of attraction, or the skeptics, start with small things so your brain can process them and make them happen. During my divorce, my initial long list of things I needed or would need included a couch, living room chairs, a dining room table and chairs, two beds, a desk and dresser for my daughter, a lawn mower, and a washer and dryer. I had a moment of panic when I started adding up the cost of those things. I realized my stinkin' thinkin' wasn't going to help my situation and stopped. Instead, I focused on how great it would feel to walk into my new living room with a beautiful couch and chairs and how peaceful it would feel as I put my feet up after a long day of moving. My daughter and I knew we wanted a blue and gray color palette in the new house, so I kept picturing how great everything would look. I saw myself folding laundry in my new utility room that wasn't stuck down in the basement but in a bright happy room. I turned my moment of panic around quickly and focused and assumed I already had the things on my desired list.

When I am manifesting things, I talk to friends and family and share with them what I need and that I am bringing those things to myself. I think initially they might have thought I was a little crazy when I would say I was working on manifesting something in particular. Then, as I was manifesting things, I started hearing, "You're so lucky, things seem to fall in your lap."

At one of my initial meetings with my realtor, Linda, we were talking about what kind of house I wanted and what my "have to have" items were and things that I could compromise on.

"I am going to need a bunch of furniture for the house," I said.

"What exactly are you going to need?" Linda asked.

I recited my list. "A couch, living room chairs, two beds, a washer, dryer, a desk and a dresser for Rachel."

All of a sudden, her face lit up, and she told me, "I have another client who is downsizing, selling their house in Michigan and all of the furniture." She said her client had posted pictures of the furniture online and asked, "Do you want to take a look?"

I said, "Yes, of course."

Linda pulled the site up online and showed me two beautiful living room chairs in the blue and gray color palette we wanted.

I asked, "Can we look at them now?"

My realtor called her client, who was home and just lived down the street. We jumped in the car, drove down the street, and met Sue, my realtor's client. Sue also had a couch that went with the two chairs, all of which were top of the line name brand and beautiful. Sue also had a queen bed and frame in her guest room that no one slept on and a desk she would throw in for my daughter. The miracles piled up that day.

All the furniture at Sue's house were the colors I wanted and what I would have picked out in the store for less than what one of the chairs would have cost new. We made a deal she would keep the furniture until her house sold or until I found my new house and was ready to move in. It was the perfect arrangement. This was in March, and I had no place to store the furniture and wasn't sure when I would be able to buy my house. As it turned out, Sue's house sold in September, and she needed the furniture out of her Michigan house the first week in October. I ended up finding my house in late September and rented it starting in October. The furniture went perfectly with my house, which I ended up buying in December after it had gone through probate.

This was a series of miracles in that my realtor's client had the furniture I needed and was able to keep the furniture while she showed her house, which saved me money and the hassle of having to find a storage unit. That the furniture was in the color palette we wanted and ended up going with the colors in my house, which I didn't know at the time I bought the furniture, is all amazing. Having faith that things will work out the way they are supposed to makes the whole LOA process happen much easier. I know some friends and family thought I was off my rocker buying furniture before I even had a house.

After my realtor had helped me find my house, we were in the negotiating stage, and she called me and asked, "Lisa, do you still need a washer and dryer?"

I replied, "I haven't found or purchased a set yet."

Linda said, "I have another client who is moving and had planned to leave the old washer and dryer in the house they were selling. They decided they would rather give the set to someone who needed it than the people who were purchasing their home because they had a set they were bringing. You will need to pick up the washer and dryer to get it to your new house."

I just had to borrow a truck and get someone help to pick up the washer and dryer and take it to my new home. Again, the timing couldn't have been better. I had possession of my home and was able to take my "new" washer and dryer directly there rather than having to store the set somewhere. The miracles keep happening.

I now needed to focus on manifesting the furniture for my daughter's room. As my daughter Rachel and I were talking about what she needed, she told me, "Mom, Maddy (her friend) found a dresser for me and is painting it for my room."

Again, I was blown away by the kindness. Maddy's parents had been divorced several years earlier, and she was trying to make it easier for Rachel. Such a good friend. So, now I needed to manifest a bed. At that point, I was prepared to buy her something, but the Universe came through with another little miracle.

I was working out with my friend who owns a fitness studio and is a personal trainer. We were talking about the divorce, and she asked, "What else do you need for your house?"

I replied, "I still need a bed for Rachel."

Her face lit up, and she told me, "My fiancé is moving in with me, and I need to get rid of my extra bedroom set so he can use that room as his office. You can have the bed and nightstand." I was overwhelmed with how blessed I am with such good friends. Another little miracle checked off my desire list.

When I moved into my house, my daughter and I had to adjust and work together to handle having only one bathroom. My daughter is a little poky in the bathroom, and I wanted to figure out somewhere in the house where we could do our hair and makeup so the other person could get in the bathroom. My initial idea was to find a vanity table and chair for my bedroom. So, I added a vanity table to my desire list and started focusing on how great it would be to have a place to get ready in the morning so neither my daughter nor I would be rushed or stressed before we left the house. I was looking online for used furniture, and before I had even told my friends I was looking for a vanity, a friend texted me a picture of an upright entertainment center her mom was getting rid of and asked if I had any interest in the piece.

A lightbulb went off in my head, and I said, "Yes, I would be very interested."

I figured that instead of a vanity table with little or no storage, this entertainment center would be a stand-up vanity with lots of storage as a plus. I painted the piece to match my bedroom colors, put an electric mirror on one of the shelves, and had lots of storage too. The piece had a cut-out for the cord for the makeup mirror. This manifestation worked out better than I had hoped, and the piece was tall and balanced the furniture in my bedroom.

Keep the faith, make your list of things you want to manifest, and picture and think about the things on your list as if you already have them. Use all your senses when thinking about those desired things. How will the item look, feel, smell, and add joy to your life? Imagine all those things and know you can manifest what you want and desire.

There were three lawn mowers in the house when my realtor took me to the showing—two riding lawn mowers and one push lawn mower. I did not have a mower and would need one to take care of the lawn at my new house. I kept focusing on a lawn mower and thinking about it often in a positive light. I also got this feeling that everything would work out, so I wasn't panicking about it. I just kept thinking about it often and in a positive light. I imagined how it would feel to smell the freshly cut grass and how satisfied I would be to see my lawn with the nice neat, new cut lines. Lastly, I thought about how it would feel to walk barefoot across my green velvety lawn. I didn't want to buy a lawnmower and just kept thinking and knowing one would turn up.

I even told my sister that maybe the previous owner of my house would leave a mower for me. Guess what? They did. So, I crossed the lawnmower off my desire list and counted it as another one of my million little miracles. The Universe delivers. We just have to ask, be clear on what we want, and not worry about how things will happen. I call it faith in having the ability to know things will work out and often even better than we imagined.

MANIFESTING PEOPLE

"As you know, like attracts like. If you want better people in your life, you must work on being a better person yourself."

—LEON BROWN

Have you ever met someone just when you needed them? You were probably practicing the law of attraction without even knowing it. Think of that person and about all of things that fell into place for you to actually meet them. Manifesting people sounds like a strange statement. What I mean by manifesting people is by bringing people in your life that you need to either teach you something or to help you with something. The process for attracting people into your life is basically the same as attracting things you want. We talked about attracting a romantic interest into your life earlier in the book. This chapter deals with attracting people of a non-romantic interest.

When I manifest people into my life, it usually starts with something I need help with that is not in my wheelhouse of expertise. For example, when I realized I was getting a divorced, I needed to find an attorney. Since I had only been married once, I didn't have a divorce attorney in my list of contacts. I knew of a divorce attorney who lived across the lake but didn't know what kind of reputation he had. I called a friend who is an attorney and had been divorced several years ago to see if she had anyone she would recommend and if she knew the attorney across the lake.

She gave me the name of her attorney but wasn't sure she was taking new clients at the time. She also thought my attorney had a great reputation and was fair. I called her attorney, who wasn't taking new clients but gave me the name of the attorney across the lake and two more attorneys. I called the other two attorneys. One wasn't taking new clients and recommended the attorney across the lake. The other was more worried about collecting her retainer than finding out what I needed and didn't leave a good impression with me. I ended up calling the attorney across the lake and had a great initial consultation. I felt like he would be helpful and had my best interest. Having an attorney who was recommended by several people was a good feeling. During the divorce process, he counseled me to not proceed a certain way that would have made him money, cost me money, and would not make a difference in the outcome of my divorce.

On a side note, my daughter won a scholarship that was set-up in his deceased mom's name the year before. My attorney's mom was a philanthropist and educator, and she had a personality that could fill a room in a positive way. She had the unique ability to make each person in that room feel like she was talking directly to them. She was truly an amazing woman. A scholarship fund had been created in her honor through a local credit union. My daughter applied and was awarded one of those scholarships. I don't think that was a coincidence.

How can you manifest people into your life? First, figure out what you need help with, what you need to learn, or who you need to help you or do something for you. Make a list of what you're looking for, the characteristics of the person you want, and any other important details. Once again, don't be afraid to ask for help or let your people know you're looking for someone to help you. You probably have one or several people in your life who are like a walking Google directory. Stay connected with those people.

I also like to ask the Universe to bring me people who I can trade services with. Since I own a marketing business, I try to manifest, for example, a landscaper who needs help with their social media. That way, I don't have to put out any cash and can get help landscaping my yard.

Take a few minutes and think about something you need help with. If you had a certain person you could ask questions or ask for help, who would that be?

I need help with

_____

_____

This person knows about (what topic) and would be willing to help me

_____

_____

I could help that person with

_____

_____

Another example happened when I needed to sell my condo in Illinois to purchase a new home in Michigan. I had owned my condo in Illinois for twenty years with a couple of long-term tenants and hadn't done very much updating other than new appliances. I was concerned because the pandemic had made finding a good contractor who wasn't booked for months nearly impossible. I also didn't know a realtor in Illinois around my condo, and I found out I would need a real estate attorney too. I wasn't sure if I would have to update the condo, which could have included painting, flooring, cabinets, and more. I watch the HGTV decorating shows but am in no way a decorating or rehabbing expert. My first concern was about how I would find these experts and, with the pandemic, how I would be able to get the work done out of state in a timely manner. And how I would supervise or manage the work?

My friend Sara called me to check on how I was doing while moving through the divorce process. I was telling her I would need to sell my condo and wasn't sure how I was going to manage the rehab work, find a realtor, and the whole process of selling the condo out of state.

"I can help you with that," Sarah said, without pausing.

She had been in the real estate business before having her kids, knew the market, and had been rehabbing property since then. She offered to go with me to look at the condo to see what I would need to do to get it ready to sell. She also put together a list of questions to ask local realtors to see if they were active, professional, and were able to get properties sold quickly. She coached me through the calls with several local realtors and helped me select the realtor I ended up using. She also offered her handyman if I needed to rehab the condo. Fortunately, after speaking with the realtor, it was determined that no rehab would be needed.

Sara was there when I needed an expert and was able to coach me through getting the condo sold. My realtor was great, answered my questions and calls, and was very responsive and professional. After my tenants moved out, I received a call from my realtor that the tenants had destroyed the carpet and it would be necessary to replace the flooring before we put the condo on the market.

Again, because of the pandemic, I was concerned I wouldn't be able to find flooring and, even more important, that I wouldn't be able to find someone who could install the flooring quickly. The tenants had moved out, so I had no rental income, I was still paying the mortgage, and I needed to get the condo sold so I could buy my house in Michigan. I was also living with my soon-to-be-ex until we agreed on the divorce terms, which was not your ideal living situation!

I took a couple of deep, calming breaths, then turned those momentary panicked thoughts into thoughts of finding inexpensive flooring and an honest contractor who could install quickly. I made several calls, which didn't help my thoughts, but kept taking those deep calming breaths. Finally, I found a chain store where I could pick out flooring locally and then have it delivered to the store in Illinois. They had a list of recommended contractors. The first contractor I called said he would have time to install the flooring the following week and would pick it up at the store for me. Again, several little miracles to add to my growing list. When those little miracles happened, I took a minute to offer up a thank you for the miracles the Universe delivered and might have done a couple of serious fist pumps too.

Another little miracle happened when I was talking with my divorce attorney about how things were going with the sale of the condo in Illinois. I explained that I had found a realtor and was in the process of replacing the flooring so we could get the condo listed and that I still needed to find a real estate attorney in Illinois. Wait for it… another little miracle. My divorce attorney said his cousin was a real estate attorney in the Chicago suburbs near where my condo was located. I contacted him, had a conversation, and hired him to handle the sale of my condo. He was also great, professional, responsive, and made the whole process very easy.

What are you doing to keep yourself moving up the emotional scale? Step out of your comfort zone and try something you don't normally do. Put on your favorite music from your high school years and have a one-person dance party. Try a new group exercise class. Skip down the street. Try something new that will make you smile.

This week to help me move up the emotional scale I am going to

_____

Another way to improve your mood and move up the emotional scale is to make an effort to help someone else. You want to be that person who makes others feel important and better about themselves. When you walk into a room of people, what level of energy do you bring to the group? There are many ways to be that person who people want to be around. Below is a list of possible ideas for you to consider:

1. Volunteer at a senior living community.
2. Offer to go into an elementary school and read to a student who could use some extra attention.
3. Mow your elderly neighbor's yard.
4. Offer to help your parents with a big project they have been putting off.
5. Volunteer at a local food bank or shelter.
6. Do something nice anonymously. Pay for the person's order behind you in a drive-up line. This type of action sends lots of good feelings into the Universe. Often the person who you bought for will do the same thing for the person behind them. That action just multiplies, and think of how everyone is pleasantly surprised from your one little kind gesture.

I believe that when we do things to help people without being asked, those good deeds will come back to us at some point. Often people label those good fortune things as being lucky. I truly believe those good things coming back to us are signs from the Universe that we are on the right track.

This week I will help

_____

_____ by offering to

_____

_____.

Earlier in the Manifesting Things chapter, I had manifested a washer and dryer with the help of my realtor and her clients. My realtor said I would need to go pick up the washer and dryer in the next couple of days from the home her clients were selling. Once again, I found myself needing help, specifically someone with a truck. My divorced girlfriend had a serious bad-ass pickup truck and agreed to help me pick up the washer and dryer. The location was between her work and the city we both lived in, so we agreed to meet after work the following day. We arrived at the house and were able to lift the dryer into her truck with no problem. The washer was heavier, and I thought we might have to go recruit someone off the street to help us. Fortunately, the previous owner and the buyer's realtor pulled into the driveway as we were figuring out how we were going to get the washer loaded into the back of the truck. They offered to help us, and within a few minutes we were on the road and headed to my new home. More little miracles were continuing to come to me just when I needed them. I offered up a serious thank you to the Universe and to the people popping into my life when I needed them.

My new home was built in 1957, and I find myself needing lots of experts and help with repairs and fix-it jobs. Before I purchased my home, the previous owner had hired a handyman to rehab the house. I'm not sure how handy the handyman really was. My first clue is that he drywalled over the dryer vent. Well, now I had to find someone who could install the manifested washer and dryer. The other part of the problem was that the original vent was vented into the garage, not the ultimate choice in Michigan.

Once again, my girlfriend had an answer to my prayer of finding a reliable handyman who knew how to fix things. She said, "My neighbor Mike has a fireplace installation business and knows how to fix anything, and I think he would help you." She went the extra step and called him. Mike agreed to meet us at my house to see what was involved in the installation.

She wasn't kidding when she told me Mike could fix anything. He met us at the house, helped us unload the machines, and looked at the vent situation. He recommended cutting a new hole in the wall that was close to the floor for the dryer vent rather than knocking a hole in the wall above where the previous one had been. This way, I wouldn't have to patch and paint around the hole, and cosmetically it would be a cleaner project. So, not only was a great handyman manifested, but he knew how to solve and fix problems others created. Mike and his son were at my house the next day to cut the new hole for the dryer vent and were able to install the washer and dryer for me. The miracles kept happening.

Also, earlier in the Manifesting Things chapter, I told the story of how the Universe brought me a lawn mower. Well, the lawnmower was a John Deere tractor that would start only if I sprayed starter fluid on the engine. I also had no idea how to drive a riding lawn mower. As a kid, I mowed lots of lawns, but we had a push lawn mower. The thought of jumping on a riding lawnmower with no instruction was a little scary. So, I went to work manifesting someone to help me get the lawnmower ready to ride and give me a lesson or two on driving the thing. It was early April, and lawn mowing season in Michigan was fast approaching.

As the weather warmed up, I started walking my dog outside, enjoying the spring days. I kept myself moving up the emotional scale and thinking about bringing someone who could help me with the lawnmower. I met my girlfriend for a drink, and we were chatting about life. I mentioned I had inherited a riding lawn mower and needed to find someone who could give it a tune-up and that I needed to figure out how to drive the machine.

She told me, "My dad is retired and loves fixing things. I will see if he can help you."

The next day, her dad, Skip, called and said, "Lisa, I will be happy to take a look at your lawn mower and give it a tune-up."

I asked, "Can you show me how to drive the machine too?"

He replied, "Of course." We made plans for the lawn-mower rehab appointment later in the week.

Skip not only looked at the lawnmower, but he also gave it a complete overhaul. He fixed the carburetor, sharpened the blades, repaired the starter, changed the oil, and reinforced the engine cover. The machine purred when he was done. He also gave me a very thorough lesson on how to operate the mower and made me practice mowing the front lawn, including how to maneuver around the ditches. I am sure the neighbors thought I was crazy as Skip filmed me mowing the yard as I gave a big thumb's up sign. A bonus miracle was that Deb, his partner, offered to split some of her perennial plants, which I gladly accepted. Another series of little miracles to add to my growing list.

Manifesting the right people into your life can make things so much easier, fun, and interesting. The people you need will help you solve problems, teach you things, and generally get things done that have been missing or needed in your life. Again, focus on what you want, not what you don't want. Act as if the person you need is already in your life, and use your senses to think how it will feel to have that person helping you with whatever you have been focusing on. Continue working toward that feeling of joy, which will make manifesting everything easier.

EIGHT THINGS I'VE LEARNED ABOUT THE LAW OF ATTRACTION

―――

"Learning never exhausts the mind."

—LEONARDO DA VINCI

Mastering the law of attraction is like learning yoga in that it is an ongoing endeavor. In yoga, you are learning new positions and mastering the basics first, and in the LOA, you are implementing the physical things to keep your head thinking positive thoughts. With both subjects, the more I practice, the more I realize the priority is about how and what I think. The important part is that it doesn't matter where anyone else is in their journey; rather, it is my journey for both subjects. Both require physical activity, the ability to think, and the process of learning to change the way I think. Over the last fifteen years, I have learned and continued to grow in my knowledge of the law of attraction. The eight most important things I have learned from practicing the law of attraction are:

1. *The kinder I am to myself and the more I love myself, the easier it is to love everything else.*

I can't talk to myself negatively and be in a joyful frame of mind. So, I am continually working on being kind to myself. I stop that voice that pops up and says I'm not doing enough when I want to take a break and rest. Instead of focusing on features I would like to change, I focus on things I am good at and do well. I think most people are really trying to do their best, including me. So, give yourself and others the benefit of the doubt and put kindness out into the world, which also includes being kind to yourself.

> "Accept yourself, love yourself, and keep moving forward. If you want to fly, you have to give up what weighs you down."
>
> —ROY T. BENNETT

2. *I can now stop myself when a negative thought pops into my head and reframe that thought into something positive.*

According to Elizabeth Scott, PhD, in her article, "The Toxic Effects of Negative Self-Talk," she states, "Those who find themselves frequently engaging in negative self-talk tend to be more stressed. This is in large part because their reality is altered to create an experience where they don't have the ability to reach the goals they've set for themselves." One of the most obvious drawbacks of negative self-talk is that it's not positive. This sounds simplistic, but research has shown that positive self-talk is a great predictor of success. For example, one study on athletes compared four different types of self-talk (instructional, motivational, positive, and negative) and found that positive self-talk was the greatest predictor of success. People didn't need to remind themselves how to do something as much as they needed to tell themselves they are doing something great and that others notice it as well (Scott 2022).

We all have bad days and bad things that happen to us. The key is how we react to those bad things. I now recognize when I start thinking negatively about something that happened. I then stop, tell myself we aren't taking the negative detour, and turn that thought into the question, *What is the lesson I am supposed to learn here?* This stops my brain from taking the negative detour and stops one negative thought leading to another, which in turn stops my whole day from going the wrong way. I also try to take a few moments to take a couple of deep breaths, which automatically starts to calm me down. Then, I focus on ten things I am grateful for right at that second.

That simple act stops the negative thoughts and starts my brain thinking positively. I feel like I am constantly giving myself little pep talks throughout the day. By really focusing on the little things in life that bring me joy, I keep my head in a good spot.

I was sitting outside on a beautiful day late in May in Michigan, writing this chapter. I was wondering how I was going to find the time to finish the first draft of my manuscript and started to feel panic set in. I stopped myself, closed my eyes, took five slow, deep breaths, and then used all of my senses to think about what I was grateful for in that moment. The sound and feel of a gentle warm wind, the birds chirping, my dog sitting right next to me, the flowers I had planted the day before. Before I had thought of my ten things I was grateful for, I felt a calm come over me and a smile spread across my face. I knew I would get the first draft of the manuscript done in time and moved on to finish the chapter.

> *"Don't be a victim of negative self-talk—
> remember you are listening."*
>
> —BOB PROCTOR

3. It is okay and important to reduce the amount of time or even eliminate contact from negative people to live my best life.

This statement sounds a little harsh, but sometimes we need to let people go. I had a friend who had gone through a breakup with a guy she had dated on and off for some time. He had been honest with her that he didn't want a committed relationship, and they had developed a pattern of her wanting more, then breaking off the relationship. She would get depressed, and it had become a vicious cycle. She would want me to listen to her analyze the situation. I tried to help and explained that she deserved better but had to like herself well enough to either not put up with this situation and find someone else or accept the situation and not let it affect her mental health. She wouldn't do either, and I couldn't keep listening to the same story over and over and over again. She needed to go back to number one on this list and work at loving herself. I couldn't do that for her. She had to do that herself, and I felt all her negativity and depression was pulling me down. I was blunt and told her she needed to have more respect for herself. She didn't like the comment and hasn't called me since. I would have liked to have been able to help her, but sometimes we must let a relationship go for our own mental health, and that is okay. We have one life to live, and we can't make people do what they should.

4. *I am not responsible for other's thoughts and actions, only my own.*

I used to spend too much time worrying about what everyone thought and not taking the time to think about what I thought or wanted with a particular situation. I tend to be the peacekeeper or relationship manager between people, and frankly, that can get exhausting. I am still a work in progress on this one, but when someone is gossiping or talking about someone else, I try to throw a positive comment in the conversation or change the topic to something more positive. If gossiping starts, I try to think about what I would say if the person who was the topic at the moment was sitting next to me. This stops me adding to the negative gossip and turns the conversation in a positive direction.

5. *When something happens that first seems like a negative, it often is the Universe clearing a path for something good headed my way.*

This took a little bit longer to learn than some of the other items on the list. I have a list of things and people I want and am manifesting. Sometimes something happens that initially seems to be a bad thing that later, looking back, needed to happen so the really good thing could happen.

An example was when I had obtained what initially appeared to be a good account for my business. Several months in, I realized it was not a good fit, the business owner wasn't paying my invoices on time, and it was taking more time than we had originally discussed for a variety of reasons. He decided he wanted to hire a large agency to handle his account. Initially I was upset, because I don't like to lose accounts. But it wasn't a great fit, he was having financial difficulties, and I wasn't getting paid in a timely fashion. Instead of being upset, I realized the Universe was clearing that account so that I would have room and time for new accounts that would be a better fit for my business. What happened was that I obtained four new accounts that were a better fit and not as high maintenance as the account I had lost. The key is not to completely freak out when something bad happens and to realize it is often just a way to make room for what you really want and have asked for.

6. *Giving back with an open heart and not expecting anything in return will bring good things back to my life.*

I think the more we can help others, the more good things come back to us. Call it karma or whatever you want, but

I truly believe the Universe delivers good things when we deliver good things. One of my clients had referred a woman to me who ran an organization that bought lemon drop candy and then donated the candy to cancer treatment centers in Southeast Michigan. Apparently, lemon drop candy made with real lemon juice has been shown to help cancer patients with their salivary glands by increasing salivation flow due to excessive radiation and chemotherapy treatment. She raised funds to buy the lemon drops and then worked with groups of kids to decorate the candy jars and delivered them to the cancer treatment centers. The woman wanted help with a logo for the group and a marketing piece design. She was more than willing to pay for the work, but I did not have the heart to charge her for either the logo or the marketing piece design. My friend designed the logo, also free of charge, and I created the marketing piece. The woman was so grateful she wrote a great Google review for me, and within a week I had gotten two new clients from referrals. If everyone would make it a priority to give back, the world would be a much kinder place.

I was amazed at how kind people were as I moved through my divorce. I have two stories I will remember forever. The first happened one month after I had found out I was going to be getting a divorce. I went to the branch manager at my financial institution to tell her what was going on and to ask for some advice about my accounts. She was very kind and told me to call her if I had any other questions. About a week later, on a rough day, I received a handwritten note in the mail from my banker. The note said, *Lisa, you are strong, you are courageous, you are brave and beautiful. You will get through this.* Needless to say, I bawled. I was floored by her thoughtfulness. It still brings tears to my eyes as I write this paragraph. I cannot express how much those words meant to me on that day and to this day.

The second story of kindness came from my landscaper, Nacho. He and his crew had been mowing our yard for years. They do a great job, and I had referred him to several neighbors. I caught Nacho on lawn mowing day at the old house and told him about the upcoming divorce and how I would pay him through that month and then my soon-to-be-ex would handle the bill. I also told him I was moving in October and didn't think I would need him at the new house. He asked where I was moving, and I told him my new address. He looked me straight in the eye and asked, "Do you need help moving?" He offered to bring his trucks and crew and help me move. Again, I was floored by the kindness offered. We find what we are looking for. If we focus on kindness, it comes right back to us in amazing ways.

In an *Insider* article by Lauren Schumacker, she lists ten ways giving back can benefit both your mental and physical self. She cited a report the Women's Philanthropy Institute noted that people are happier overall when they give to others and that the more they do or give, the happier they tend to be. It's simply referred to as "the joy of giving." From lowering your depression levels to lowering blood pressure, giving back has a positive impact on both the person giving and the people or the organization receiving. So, a great way to improve your mood is to volunteer or help someone. The benefits are a blessing to both parties (Schumacker 2018).

> *"The best way to find yourself is to lose yourself in the service of others."*
>
> —MAHATMA GANDHI

7. Learning is a life-long process.

The law of attraction concept is intellectually fairly easy to understand. Like attracts like. Putting that into practice is a continual learning process. According to an article from Healthline.com, the average person has over 6,000 thoughts per day (Raypole 2022). That is quite a few chances to think positively. With that many thoughts every day, I have learned I need to keep practicing and learning how to use the law of attraction to my advantage by thinking positively, asking for what I want, and then knowing or having the faith the Universe will deliver.

8. Affirmations are a way to increase my vibrational level.

Saying affirmations daily works to increase my vibrational level. I have learned by focusing on positive things and thinking as if I already have what I am trying to manifest, I am closer to joy, gratitude, and appreciation, which are emotions on the higher end of the scale. The higher my vibrational level, the closer I am to manifesting what I want.

In the Cleveland Clinic's Health Essentials December 7, 2021, blog, psychologist Lauren Alexander, PhD, explains how daily positive affirmations can help you face the world with a belief in yourself and your abilities. Alexander shares the following tips:

1. Practice being positive.
2. Put skepticism on hold.
3. Say the affirmations aloud or to yourself.
4. Pair your affirmations with action (Cleveland Clinic 2021).

I think number four is an important practice for the law of attraction. We can't just wish for something and not put any sort of action plan into place. Wanting something paired with an action plan will make it happen.

> *"It's the repetition of affirmations that leads to belief. And once that belief becomes a deep conviction, things begin to happen."*
>
> —MUHAMMAD ALI

CHOOSE JOY

"Joy does not simply happen to us. We have to choose joy and keep choosing it every day."

—HENRI J.M. NOUWEN

We all go through difficult times during our life. Sometimes I marvel at how some people can move forward despite having been through a traumatic event such as losing a child to suicide. Kris Miller, founder of On a Dragonfly's Wings, is one of those people.

Kris and her husband, Joe, lost their fifteen-year-old son, Nikolai, to suicide on June 20, 2019. Nikolai was one of those kids who lit up the room with his smile and the sparkle in his eyes. Nikolai had a difficult freshman year of high school and had slowly been withdrawing from things and activities he had always enjoyed in the past. Kris and Joe were concerned about Nikolai and sought assistance from therapists, school counselors, and teachers. However, despite their efforts, Nikolai took his own life.

There were a few signs that something was amiss the night of June 20; however, it didn't occur to Kris until after Nikolai's death. For one thing, when Kris arrived home from work that fateful night, the kitchen was clean, which was unusual. Those of us with teenagers can relate. Usually, she walked into the kitchen to a sink of dirty dishes from her three boys' breakfast, lunch, and snacks for the day. Nikolai had cleaned up the kitchen prior to her return from work. And while Kris had a quick dinner prior to an event that evening, and Nikolai asked if she wanted to have ice cream with him. She told him they would have ice cream together after her event.

While at the event, Kris received the call that no parent should ever receive. Her oldest son called and said she needed to get home. Nikolai had died by suicide. In my mind, there can be nothing worse than losing your child to suicide. Absolutely nothing.

According to the American Foundation for Suicide prevention in 2020, there were 1.2 million suicide attempts in the US, and 45,979 Americans lost their lives to suicide (American Foundation for Suicide Prevention 2022).

Kris and her husband were aware of their son's struggle, took steps to help him, and still lost their son.

I asked Kris, "How did you not just curl up in bed and stay there?"

Her answer was that she had a husband and two other children who needed her. She said it was about two weeks after Nikolai's suicide when it finally hit her.

She had been so busy doing all the things you have to do when someone passes that the loss hadn't really sunk in. At that time, she started to feel the weight of her grief, and it became all consuming, until she started to notice dragonflies. Whenever she was in deep grief and needed comfort, dragonflies started showing up. Kris knew instantly this was Nikolai letting her know he was okay. In a mind shift, she started thinking more about Nikolai's life than his death. He was pure joy. His whole life was spent choosing and spreading joy. This is when Kris realized that choosing joy was how she was going to push through even her deepest grief. In addition, she made the decision to find a way to honor Nikolai's memory by educating people about suicide and the signs to watch for so that no other parent would have to go through the horror of losing their child.

With the help of many, Kris formed a non-profit called On a Dragonfly's Wings. The mission of the organization is "to provide emotional support by sharing experiences, for survivors of suicide loss and individuals with lived experience with suicide, while engaging in community prevention through mental health education and public policy advocacy to support a healthier future" (OnADragonFlysWings.com).

Kris has taken the absolute worst experience in her life and redirected all those negative thoughts to help others. She has bad days and gives herself permission to grieve. Her one rule is that she can't lay in bed all day. She must get up. This helps acknowledge her feelings of grief while not allowing herself to be consumed by them. Getting up and spending time in nature helps move her up that emotional scale.

Despite experiencing the devastating loss of her son, Kris has chosen joy. Our mindset is a daily decision. I hope Kris's story is an inspiration to the rest of us that our mindset is a choice and to pick joy, peace, and happiness.

Changing the way you think, focusing on loving yourself, and living a joyful life everyday will put you in the perfect position to manifest all your dreams. "Like attracts like" is the main premise behind the law of attraction. If your thoughts are going to attract things, doesn't it make more sense to think positive thoughts?

You have the tools to start manifesting exactly what you desire, right now. The more you practice the law of attraction, the easier it will become to bring those things you want to yourself. Keep your vibrational level at the top of the emotional scale by thinking positively and focusing only on what you want in an optimistic way. Make sure you are taking care of yourself by eating healthy, hydrating, and sleeping. Take the time in the morning when you first wake up to set the tone for the day in your mind. Think of those things you are grateful for, and use all your senses to think about how it will feel, look, hear, and smell like when your dreams become your reality. Thank the Universe for delivering.

I was thinking of things that make me smile, and dancing is one of those things. I am not a good dancer, but I have never been angry on a dance floor. It is hard not to smile when you are dancing to your favorite song, with or without friends. Crank your favorite music and dance like nobody is watching. If dancing isn't your thing, think of an activity you love to do that makes you smile. Do more of that thing!

The next step is to put together a plan of action that will move you toward the thing you're trying to manifest. While putting your action plan into place, have faith the Universe will deliver, and be open to opportunities that may deliver something even better than what you're trying to manifest. Know the Universe is working for you.

You might find certain steps in the process easier than other steps. Based on my experience, reading, and putting the law of attraction into practice, I think the most important part of the process is keeping yourself up on the vibrational scale. Again, my common sense thinking is that if you're happy with yourself, you will be happier about everything else too. When I was not happy with me, I struggled, especially with my energy level and my relationships. If you're depressed, angry, or feeling rage, it is going to be more difficult to manifest the good things you desire.

My journey with the law of attraction has been a journey of self-preservation and hope. We all go through the ups and downs of life. When you're in one of those valleys life throws at you, the law of attraction can provide that glimmer of hope or the faint light in the future that things will get better. When I first began to hear and learn about the law of attraction, I was grasping at anything that could help me get through one of those rough patches.

Things were grim. I wasn't happy with myself, and that was oozing out into the other parts of my life. The journey begins with learning to love yourself first. You can't control what other people do or say, so it all starts within your own head. That can be a hard pill to swallow, and it is much easier to blame someone or something else for your problems.

The little glimmer of hope is what I want to provide to those reading this book. Things will get better, you will make it through this rough patch, and the law of attraction is a tool for you to use indefinitely to make the rough patches smoother, your life more joyful, and the ups and downs not as extreme. It is like when people are talking about an eating plan not being a diet but a lifestyle.

We really, really need to be ultra-aware of the things we are saying and thinking. I had dinner last night with a friend who spent the first half hour of our conversation complaining about how stressed he was. Later in the evening, he went on to say he is a positive person. Our dialogue with ourselves is so important. I struggle more with what I am thinking and the things I am saying to myself. Don't beat yourself up, but as you put the activities into place, you will catch yourself when you are speaking negatively and can redirect your thoughts. Start your morning with seventeen full seconds of gratitude and happy thoughts before any negative thoughts can creep into your brain. Then move to your gratitude journal and write down what you are grateful for that morning before you get out of bed.

You will stumble, and that is part of learning something new. Don't get down on yourself. Jump back into the positive parade and do something you love or brings you joy. Find the joy in the little everyday things, like the sun shining or a smile from a stranger. Take a page from your dog, and be happy all the time. I would love to bottle the joy my dog exudes when I come home from being gone. He is so darn happy, it is contagious. Be a viral spreader of happiness and joy. What you put out in the Universe comes back to you.

There are many benefits of focusing on keeping your head right and moving yourself up the vibrational scale. First, you will find yourself happier more often. Happy thoughts bring more happy thoughts. You will learn to be grateful or more grateful for everything you currently have. You will also learn to reframe things and shift your perspective from negative to positive. It becomes much easier to shift or redirect your thoughts when you hit a bump in the road. I find that when something bad happens now, which might have sent me into a tailspin in the past, I can recognize the situation isn't ideal but also realize I am supposed to learn a lesson and not give the bad thing more negative attention. You will also accomplish more goals and live your best life by making your dreams come true. You will have days or periods where it feels like great things are just plopping into your life faster than you can imagine.

By reading, stating, and writing affirmations daily, practicing self-care, and working at being nice to myself, I have been able to furnish most of my new home and bring people into my life who were able to help me with a variety of things. I was able to experience joy, happiness, and fun, even while going through a divorce, by practicing all the techniques in this book. I put my faith in the Universe, or, for me, God, and knew that everything would work out even better than I had imagined. My life is now one of peace, gratitude, and joy. My common sense approach to the law of attraction has always been if other people can change how they think and talk to themselves, I should be able to do the same thing. It works, people!

The world would be a much better place to live if everyone understood like attracts like and were able to put the law of attraction into practice. Once you begin, you will find that things will start working out in your favor. Those close to you will notice, and they'll say, "Things just seem to work out for you."

The law of attraction is not a quick-fix or a Band-Aid for a problem. It is a way of life, and it takes practice, which brings about those signs and synchronicities letting you know you're on the right path. Appreciate those signs for what they really are, not coincidences but little thumbs up from the Universe to keep going. You've got this. *Dream big*, and ask for what you want. Let the Universe bring it to you, and then *dream bigger!*

ACKNOWLEDGMENTS

To my sister, Lora Meier. I wouldn't have made it through the year before writing this book without you. Thanks for being my quarterback, my counselor, and for always answering the phone.

To my parents, thank you for a strong foundation on right and wrong. You lead by example and will leave the world a better place than you found it. Thank you for your unending support and always believing in me.

Thanks to my extended family for your love and support.

Thank you to my dear "old" friends. You rallied and lifted me up when I needed you most. Your check-in calls always came at the right time. I am beyond blessed you are in my life.

To my Michigan tribe, thank you for keeping my social calendar booked and busy. You provided lots of love, laughs, and support.

Thank you, Tara Ondusky, for the introduction that led me to Georgetown University's Creator Institute. Without your introduction, this book wouldn't have happened.

To Gloria Jensenius, thank you for the title of the book and your listening ear.

To my team at Creator Institute and New Degree Press, wow. You kept me on the right track and calmed me down weekly. The things I learned and the information you provided have been unbelievable. I can't imagine trying to get this book written or published without your guidance. Thank you.

To my author community, you rock! Thank you for helping me reach my pre-sale campaign goal and your words of encouragement and insights. I am beyond thankful for each of you, from new friends to reconnecting with long-term friends. I am beyond humbled for all you have done.

This book-writing journey has been one more miracle on my list and was better than I could have imagined, because of you.

Thank you!

APPENDIX

Introduction

Cherry, Kendra. 2022. "What is the Negativity Bias?" *Verywell Mind*. Accessed October 4, 2022. https://www.verywellmind.com/negative-bias-4589618.

US Department of Health & Human Services. 2020. "Marriage and Divorce." Center for Disease Control and Prevention—United States. Accessed September 29, 2022. https://www.cdc.gov/nchs/fastats/marriage-divorce.htm.

Walker, Vanessa. 2020. *Make Room for Joy: Choose Hope and Cultivate Joy in the Middle of Life's Most Complicated Seasons*. Read by Vanessa Joy Walker. TN: Carpenter's Son Publishing. Audible audio ed., 8 hr., 2 min.

What Is the Law of Attraction?

Hay, Louise. 1999. *You Can Heal Your Life*. CA: Hay House, Inc.

Hicks, Abraham. 2019. "Abraham Hicks Vibration Turn into Thoughts and Thoughts into Things." YouTube. February 22, 2019. 14:30. https://youtu.be/-hQh3GMOoMQ.

Hicks, Esther, and Jerry Hicks. 2004. *Ask and It Is Given Learning to Manifest Your Desires*. India: Hay House Publications Pvt. Ltd.

Holland, Kimberly. 2020. "Positive Self-Talk." Healthline. Accessed June 27, 2021. https://www.healthline.com/health/positive-self-talk.

Proctor, Bob. 2015. "The Law of Attraction Explained." YouTube. September 11, 2015. 7:27. https://youtu.be/5zvnFM2BXqY.

Working Scholars. 2003. "Define Universal Law." Study.com. Accessed September 29, 2022. https://homework.study.com/explanation/define-universal-law.html.

Get Your Head Right

Caren, Allie. 2018. "Why We Often Remember the Bad Better than the Good." *The Washington Post*. Accessed September 20, 2022. https://www.washingtonpost.com/science/2018/11/01/why-we-often-remember-bad-better-than-good/.

Harvard Health. 2019. "More Evidence That Exercise Can Boost Mood." *Mind & Mood* (blog), *Harvard Health Publishing*. Accessed September 29, 2022. https://www.health.harvard.edu/mind-and-mood/more-evidence-that-exercise-can-boost-mood.

Hicks, Esther, and Jerry Hicks. 2004. *Ask and It Is Given: Learning to Manifest Your Desires*. India: Hay House Publications Pvt. Ltd.

Kristenson, Sarah. 2022. "9 Science-Backed Benefits of Using Positive Affirmations." *Happier Human* (blog). Accessed September 29, 2022. https://www.happierhuman.com/benefits-affirmations/.

US Department of Health & Human Services. 2021. "Adult Obesity Facts." Center for Disease Control and Prevention—United States. Accessed September 29, 2022. https://www.cdc.gov/obesity/data/adult.html.

What Are Your Thoughts on the Law of Attraction?

Forleo, Marie. 2019. "Self-made millionaire: The simple strategy that helped increase my odds of success by 42 percent." *Make It* (blog), *CNBC*. Accessed October 16, 2022. https://www.cnbc.com/2019/09/13/self-made-millionaire-how-to-increase-your-odds-of-success-by-42-percent-marie-forleo.html.

Harvard Health Publishing. 2021. "Exercise is An All-Natural Treatment to Fight Depression." *Mind & Mood* (blog), *Harvard Health Publishing.* Accessed September 29, 2022. https://www.health.harvard.edu/mind-and-mood/exercise-is-an-all-natural-treatment-to-fight-depression.

Peale, Norman. 1959. *The Amazing Results of Positive Thinking.* New York: Ballantine Books.

Reinberg, Steven. 2022. "Depression Affects Almost 1 in 10 Americans." *US News & World Report.* Accessed September 19, 2022. https://www.usnews.com/news/health-news/articles/2022-09-19/depression-affects-almost-1-in-10-americans.

Seinfeld, Jessica. 2009. *Deceptively Delicious: Simple Secrets to Get Your Kids Eating Good Food.* New York: HarperCollins.

Coincidences, Signs, and Synchronicities

Jung, C. G. 1960. *Synchronicity: An Acausal Connecting Principle.* New Jersey: Princeton University Press.

Merriam-Webster Dictionary. 2022. "Synchronous." Springfield, MA: Merriam-Webster. https://www.merriam-webster.com/dictionary/synchronous.

Oxford Learner's Dictionaries. 2022. "Coincidence." Oxford, UK: Oxford University Press. https://www.oxfordlearnersdictionaries.com/definition/american_english/coincidence.

Thorndike, E. L., and Clarence L. Barnhart. "Coincidence." 1968. *Advanced Junior Dictionary*. IL: Scott, Foresman and Company.

How to Use the Law of Attraction—Money

Hill, Napoleon. 1960. *Think & Grow Rich*. PA: Manna Christian Outreach.

How to Use the Law of Attraction—Relationships

Sinrich, Jenn. 2020. "4 Signs Your Past Relationships Are Affecting Your Current Romance." *Wedding Wire*. October 17, 2022. https://www.weddingwire.com/wedding-ideas/past-relationships-current-romance.

The Law of Attraction and Disease

Hicks, Abraham, and Esther Hicks. 2020. "Do This Every Morning for 17 Seconds Powerful Manifestation Tool." February 22, 2020. 14:41. YouTube. https://youtu.be/RnFBz5QL9Uo.

Johns Hopkins Medicine. 2021. "The Power of Positive Thinking." *Wellness and Prevention* (blog), Johns Hopkins Medicine.

Accessed October 2, 2022. https://www.hopkinsmedicine.org/health/wellness-and-prevention/the-power-of-positive-thinking

Woods, Lisa. 2019. "3 Scientific Studies That Prove the Power of Positive Thinking." *The Startup* (blog), Medium. September 22, 2019. https://medium.com/swlh/3-scientific-studies-that-prove-the-power-of-positive-thinking-616477838555.

Eight Things I've Learned About the Law of Attraction

Cleveland Clinic. 2021. "Do Positive Affirmations Work? What Experts Say." *Health Essentials* (blog), Cleveland Clinic. Accessed October 4, 2021. https://health.clevelandclinic.org/do-positive-affirmations-work/.

Raypole, Crystal. 2022. "How Many Thoughts Do You Have Per Day and Other Things to Think About." Healthline. Accessed October 2, 2022. https://www.healthline.com/health/how-many-thoughts-per-day.

Schumacker, Lauren. 2018. "10 Ways Giving Back Can Benefit Your Mental and Physical Health." *Insider*. https://www.insider.com/how-giving-back-can-benefit-you-2018-11 (accessed October 16, 2022).

Scott, Elizabeth. 2022. "The Toxic Effect of Negative Self-Talk." Verywell Mind. Accessed October 3, 2022. https://www.verywellmind.com/negative-self-talk-and-how-it-affects-us-4161304.

Choose Joy

American Foundation for Suicide Prevention. 2022. "Suicide Statistics." American Foundation for Suicide Prevention. Accessed October 10, 2022. https://afsp.org/suicide-statistics/.

www.ingramcontent.com/pod-product-compliance
Lightning Source LLC
LaVergne TN
LVHW012025060526
838201LV00061B/4458